THE EYE OF THE TRAINER

Animal Training, Transformation, and Trust

Ken Ramirez

The Eye of the Trainer
Animal Training, Transformation, and Trust

Karen Pryor Clicker Training
Sunshine Books, Inc.
49 River Street, Suite 3
Waltham, MA 02453 USA
U. S. (Toll Free) 1-800-472-5425
781-398-0754

www.clickertraining.com

For information about special discounts for multiple-copy purchase, please contact Karen Pryor Clicker Training sales:
U. S. (Toll Free) 1-800-472-5425 or 781-398-0754 or
wholesale@clickertraining.com

Editing: Nini Bloch
Cover/book design: Lindsay Davisson
Cover photo: Choose Positive

First edition published 2020

Printed in the United States of America

ISBN-13: 978-1-890948-887

Library of Congress Control Number: 2019953013

THE EYE OF THE TRAINER

Animal Training, Transformation, and Trust

Table of Contents

Introduction

Long before I became a trainer I was fascinated with learning and behavior. That fascination led me to explore ways to improve the lives of animals through training and to investigate the nature of training itself. Through the years, I have learned that training is a transformative process for both the learner and the teacher. Critical to success in this transformation is developing trust among all involved. Without it, true collaboration and choice for the learner is not possible. Because of the shared experience and enhanced welfare that trust promotes, I look at training as an essential component of excellent animal care.

There are sets of principles, practices, perspectives, tools, and techniques that are essential to good training. For me, good training has become inextricably linked with the effective application of positive reinforcement. It embodies the ideals of trust, choice, and welfare that make great animal care possible. This collection of my writing is designed to help others see animal training through this lens, through the eye of a trainer.

Most of the articles, essays, and stories in this book were written between 2015 and 2019 for my monthly column on the Karen Pryor Clicker Training website. What I share in this book is written from the perspective of 40 years of professional training experience and reflects on a career working with a huge diversity of species—literally, thousands.

My journey to becoming a positive reinforcement trainer is unconventional. I am a "crossover" trainer. Initially, I learned to train in a guide-dog organization where punishers were an important part of the training. Later, when I started my first job as a professional trainer in a zoological facility, I was introduced to a style of training that focused on positive reinforcement.

I was fascinated to learn that large exotic animals could be trained without punishment. At that early stage in my career, I naively believed that only exotic animals could be trained solely by using positive reinforcement but that training domestic animals required the additional use of punishment. In my first two years as a trainer, I had the good fortune to work with cetaceans, sea lions, primates, big cats, and many species of birds, reptiles, and fish; in all I trained several dozen species. I remember when I came to realize that training tools worked across species—when I began training a giant Aldabra tortoise that was being destructive. I helped develop a training plan to give the tortoise an alternative activity that prevented the unwanted behavior and allowed us to reinforce him for the new activity.

As I watched that training plan work successfully, I had a flashback to my guide-dog days and realized that this type of redirection should be possible with dogs as well. Maybe punishment wasn't necessary with dogs after all! I felt foolish that I hadn't seen that sooner, but you don't know what you don't know. These experiences with so many species taught me to be adaptable, to see connections, and to vary the ways I use tools.

The next big leap in my unconventional journey came when I was thrust into a leadership position early in my career—too early! Much of my learning during my first few years as a supervisor happened through making mistakes and through trial and error. I became keenly aware of my faults and my lack of knowledge. I delved into the science of behavior change and explored various management strategies while traveling all over the world and working in some unique and exotic places, including Mexico, Japan, and French Polynesia. Those international experiences provided a learning platform to explore new teaching strategies and to work across cultures.

When I ended up at Chicago's world-class Shedd Aquarium, I helped put together a new training program, and my leadership and training skills matured. Despite lacking an advanced degree, I began teaching a graduate course on animal training at Western Illinois University, which led to the publication of my first book, *Animal Training: Successful Animal Management through Positive Reinforcement*. My experiences in Chicago opened a vast new training world to me. I became a consultant in the zoological field, developed and starred in a television training program, and ventured into the world of working-dog training, including search-and-rescue work and law-enforcement training, areas that I knew little about. I came full circle and began working again with guide-dog organizations that brought me in to help them implement positive reinforcement into their programs.

In 2014, when Karen Pryor was considering retiring, she approached me about stepping into her role overseeing the education vision and mission at Karen Pryor Clicker Training and Karen Pryor Academy. This seemed like an ideal next step for me, acknowledging my desire to find ways to make a difference and to have an impact on animal care and training around the world. In 2017, I moved to my new ranch in Washington state, to found the Karen Pryor National Training Center ("The Ranch").

My unconventional career path has brought me into a divisive pet training community, and the working-dog world is still struggling to eliminate a reliance on punishers. I continue to help zoos embrace training that is controversial because there are still those who see training as unnatural and something that belongs in a circus. We live in a time when animal welfare is a growing priority, wildlife increasingly is in peril, and the pet training world is in need of unified leadership. I find myself uniquely positioned to influence animal policy at the governmental level, animal protection in natural environments, and individual trainer practices all over the world. The essays, articles, and stories in this book reflect my perspectives on this unique training world. These stories are about training, transformation, and trust. I hope you will find them enlightening and useful to your own journey as a trainer.

Happy Training,

1

Training Matters

"Matters" here is an intentional double entendre, used both as a verb, indicating that something is important, and as a noun, meaning "material." In the first article, I address why training matters; in subsequent pieces I describe basic training concepts from my perspective, ideas that are not, in my experience, mainstream or common. I wrote each piece not for beginners but to encourage professional trainers to look at the basics with fresh eyes. I share the philosophy expressed in "Why Training Matters" at the start of every class or seminar I teach, and its concepts inform every other article in this book. Sprinkled throughout are stories about experiences that were enlightening or meaningful, including, in this chapter, "Training by Any Other Name."

Over the last few decades, the positive reinforcement community has grown and embraced new ways of looking at training. If my thought processes and perspectives have entered the mainstream, I am happy. If, as you read these articles, you think, "That's exactly how I train," you are likely in the minority. I encourage you to share these ideas widely and to help others see training from the positive perspective.

Why Training Matters

Whenever I teach a training course, I like to begin with a review of my philosophy of training and the importance of prioritizing the reasons for teaching animals and using positive reinforcement. I include this introduction and share these thoughts at the start of all new consultations. I used to be surprised by the reaction of some of my professional clients when they pushed back against my perspective and openly disagreed with me. But I now understand why they are hesitant to accept my philosophical stance, and I enjoy the challenge of bringing them around to my way of thinking. My effort starts with my standard introduction to training, which follows these key points:

Training = Teaching

I start most classes defining training with a single word: *teaching*. We teach animals how to live in our world, whether it's a dog in our home, a lion in a zoo, or a donkey in a pasture. Teaching is a natural process. Animals are always learning whether we are involved or not, so our goal is to facilitate learning and help animals navigate living among us. Although this may not be a definition that is technically accurate, I believe it is a practical one. Teaching implies a shared process, and learners must be willing participants in the process if we are going to be successful.

Training is not a luxury

In my view, there are four cornerstones that form the foundation of a professional training program. If you are missing any one of these four building blocks, you have built your program on a faulty foundation. In no particular order, these are the four cornerstones:

- *Health care program*: We must have a good relationship with a veterinary team. The health of the animal is always a top priority, so there is no way to proceed without an excellent health care program.
- *Nutrition program*: A significant part of maintaining the health of animals is providing appropriate nutrition with the right selection of proper food and vitamins.

- *Environmental program*: Since animals are directly impacted by the environment around them, we must make sure that climate, terrain, furniture, and social structure are all considered and designed in their best interest.
- *Behavioral program*: Every professional animal care program should include a training and enrichment component. Sadly, the training and enrichment component often is treated as an afterthought, something caregivers will consider if they have time. One of the reasons that millions of pets are euthanized every year in the United States alone is that owners adopt pets without recognizing the importance of good behavior management. I am still surprised that some zoos do not have a formal training program or even a position to oversee training and enrichment. Thankfully, that's changing. Training should not be considered a luxury; it is a key component to good animal care.

Primary reasons for training

It is important to prioritize the reasons that we train animals. I like to divide them into primary and secondary reasons. A primary reason for training is anything that directly benefits the individual animal in front of me—not the species, not humankind, but the animal I'm caring for right now! The three primary reasons for training described below all contribute to an animal's welfare and assure us that the animal's needs come first.

- *Physical exercise*: No matter the size of an animal's habitat—the backyard, the pasture, or the zoo enclosure—it will rarely be enough to allow the animal to exercise and get the workout that it needs. Much of a wild animal's exercise budget is taken up with the search for food, the avoidance of predators, and other things that we take care of for our animals. So, it is easy for these animals to become lazy, exercise less, and get out of shape. Training ensures that animals get a good healthy workout.
- *Mental stimulation*: Similarly, animals in our care rarely need to worry about finding a meal, avoiding predators, or searching for

appropriate temperatures, because we take care of those needs. But, without a job to do, it is easy for an animal to become bored. That's why many animals develop unwanted behaviors; they are simply looking for something to do. Training and enrichment provide activities that stimulate the brain, food puzzles require thought and foraging skills, and exercises encourage animals to run, jump, swim, fly, or play. Training lets us stimulate animals' minds in productive ways.

- *Cooperative behavior*: Finally, training lets us teach animals to participate in their own care. We can teach an animal to walk on a leash, enter a kennel when requested, present its paws for nail clipping, open its mouth for teeth brushing, and so many more cooperative behaviors. This type of training makes medical care easier and reduces the stress associated with veterinary exams for all involved.

Secondary reasons for training

There are many other good reasons to train animals, but most of them are secondary. They include education, conservation, research, entertainment, sport, work, and the list goes on. Here I was once interrupted by a zoo director, "Ken, I would include education, conservation, and research as primary reasons for training as well."

"No," I responded, "those are primary reasons for the existence of your zoo, but not primary reasons for me to have my job." I went on to explain that, although education and conservation are noble goals and ones that I support, they should not have priority over an animal's well-being. Trainers can feel compelled to push animals too far in the name of education or in the pursuit of conservation goals if those are considered primary reasons for training. That is unacceptable to me. By placing animal welfare goals ahead of the other zoological goals, it ensures animal care is the top priority. I support the role of zoos and aquariums in educating and contributing to research and conservation efforts. These are important goals, but when it comes to training, the animal's primary needs must take priority. The zoo director could not argue with that, and he allowed me to continue with my consult.

A recurring stumbling block

The example above may have been the first time that someone challenged my prioritization of training goals, but it would not be the last. I began to see great success in my work with law enforcement agencies, since I was helping them improve their use of positive reinforcement tools. During a new consult with a state K-9 unit, as I wrapped up talking about secondary reasons for training, the sergeant in charge of training quickly spoke up. "Mr. Ramirez, can we take a short break?" He and I walked into his office and he barked, "You can't tell my officers that work is a secondary reason for training! That is the *only* reason we train!"

"I understand that the work is the primary reason for your department to have dogs, but it cannot be the primary reason for training, not if I'm consulting," I replied. I could tell my answer did not sit well with him, so I offered, "You don't have to use me as a consultant. I can pack up and go home."

"No!" the sergeant quickly countered. "We want you to consult with us!"

"But, why?" I asked.

With a concerned tone he explained, "Because the other law enforcement agencies you've worked with have had such remarkable success!"

All I could do was shrug my shoulders and nod my head knowingly.

Proof is in the results

I firmly believe that putting the needs of the animal first aids in successful training. When the work task or other external training goal is set as the priority, it leads trainers to push too hard and set unrealistic expectations. When we put the animal's needs first and use positive reinforcement to achieve training goals, however, the result is a healthy and happy animal. Animals in that state are usually eager to work and end up doing exceptionally well. Instead of an animal forced to do a job, you have an animal excited to play a game. It may be serious work from the law enforcement perspective, but if the animal is having a great time and playing its favorite game, the results are an exceptional work ethic. The proof can be seen in the improved results from the many working-dog programs that have adopted this philosophy.

I know that this philosophical basis for training is not universal, but it is my training ethic. I know everyone's ethics are going to be different, and I don't expect everyone to embrace my ethics. I just want people to understand why I approach training the way I do: it produces excellent results and puts animals' needs first.

The Six Most Overlooked Fundamentals of Successful Training

As a consultant, I am asked to critique training sessions, evaluate program designs, and help solve problems. Each client presents unique challenges, whether I am helping a private client, a working-dog organization, or a zoo training program, but my suggestions for improvement tend to be the same. When I evaluate students at The Ranch or look to improve my own training, I revisit these important points time and time again.

1. Maintain an adequate rate of reinforcement.

A high rate of reinforcement can fix many problems and improve animal performance quickly. When clients use a thin schedule of reinforcement, I see animals that are confused or frustrated. Sometimes trainers use less reinforcement because they are trying to conserve food for later training, and sometimes trainers believe that experienced animals no longer need continuous reinforcement. When training starts to break down, however, rate of reinforcement is one of the first things I examine. I understand the need and desire to reduce reliance on food, but trainers must work hard to develop alternative reinforcers. With a concerted and purposeful effort, trainers can use a wide variety of reinforcers other than food; once established, these non-food reinforcers must be monitored and evaluated carefully to make sure that they remain effective.

2. Make training sessions fun.

Sometimes trainers can become so focused on the end results of their "important" training that, inadvertently, they put too much pressure on the animal to succeed. Even when the training must be serious, like training a dolphin to give a blood sample, teaching a guide dog to avoid obstacles, or training a military dog to detect explosives, the trainer should keep the session fun for the animal. The session should be interesting, engaging, and reinforcing. Intersperse the harder trials or longer durations with shorter and easier tasks that have a strong reinforcement history.

I regularly encounter trainers who lose the joy of training and transfer their tension and concern about accomplishing a critical task to their animals. No matter how serious or important the training task, making sure the animal is having fun will help the animal relax and be more successful.

3. Enrich the environment and fill the mental void in an animal's day.

Animals are always learning, not just when we have treats and a clicker in our hands. We often pay so much attention to what occurs during a training session that we forget about what the animals are doing outside of training. Training takes up only one small part of an animal's day. It is up to trainers to make sure that the remainder of the day is also set up to enrich the animals' lives. Toys, feeder puzzles, putting food in interesting places, proper social structure, opportunities to rest, ability to exercise, and locations that provide comfort and shelter from the elements are just a few of the important things that must be provided to create a safe and enriching environment. If training is the only part of the day that is stimulating, then a large part of an animal's day may be boring, which can have a huge impact on the well-being of the animal—and lead to a variety of avoidable behavioral and medical problems. I encourage trainers to be thoughtful about every aspect of an animal's day so that its mental and social needs are met. This effort will result in a healthier, more engaged animal, better training sessions, and improved overall welfare.

4. Train core behaviors as a foundation for success.

To train complex behaviors, make sure each animal has a solid foundation of fluent and regularly practiced core behaviors. These behaviors may differ for every animal and program and can include stationing, targeting, stay/wait, recall, follow, retrieve, pick it up, drop it, push it, pull it, come closer, back up, spin, and many more.

Training fluent core behaviors is helpful in several ways. This training:

- Sets up animals with the skills to learn new and more complex behaviors quickly
- Helps animals learn to use new enrichment devices and solve food puzzles more easily
- Enables the trainer to create variety in training sessions by interspersing easy core behaviors within a long, difficult, or otherwise predictable session

- Allows trainers to adjust and fine-tune behaviors by guiding the animal into the correct position or shaping their movements. For example, an animal that has a back-up cue and a hip-targeting cue can get into a new position for a medical exam quickly, something that would otherwise take a long time to train.

New core behaviors can be trained easily, and they expand an animal's repertoire quickly. These behaviors form the foundation for other behaviors. Having them in an animal's repertoire can enhance training success.

5. Read the emotional body language of animals.

It is essential that a trainer be able to read the animal's body language and respond to what the animal is experiencing. Although this tenet may seem obvious, I am often surprised when I see a trainer who either doesn't know how to interpret an animal's reactions or simply ignores what the animal is clearly indicating (see "Tiger Trust," p. 66). A big part of gaining an animal's trust and being successful as a trainer is learning to read and respond to the signals that animals exhibit. For example, a trainer should only give a cue when the animal shows it is paying attention and is ready to proceed. Trainers should be able to tell when an animal is tense or relaxed, hesitant or eager, excited or nervous, and that information should shape the trainer's decisions about next steps in each session. Experienced trainers seem to discover this truth at some point in their careers. An understanding of animal body language should be one of the first things new trainers learn because it is one of the most critical keys to providing exceptional animal care.

6. Communicate with the people involved.

Trainers understandably focus their attention on the animal's needs, sometimes not giving much thought to the human part of the equation. Being a successful animal trainer involves working with people, including coworkers, clients, and family members. Good training teams set clear training goals, agree on criteria, implement consistent protocols, and communicate from day to day. When communication systems are not in place and trainers or family members fail to talk about their training goals, progress, or setbacks, the animal suffers. If trainers don't have shared expectations of the animal's behavior, clear criteria, consistent cues, and consistent interactions from one trainer to the next, animals can receive conflicting information and find training sessions confusing and frustrating. In addition, leaders, consultants, and teachers can only be successful with employees, clients, and students if they are good communicators. Clear communication develops trust among the human members of the training team, and everyone benefits, including the animal.

Animals come first

There are certainly far more aspects to successful training than I have articulated here. However, I have selected these six principles because they are the most common. When I am called in as a consultant, I can usually count on one or more of these aspects being neglected or forgotten.

I firmly believe that the animal's needs should always come first. When trainers improve their training and use the principles discussed above, they come closer to making the lives of animals better. I am hopeful that you find this list useful, and that an idea or tip might make your training more effective.

Something Borrowed, Something True: Eight of My Favorite Sayings

There are plenty of maxims, adages, and popular sayings in the training community. I tend to avoid them, because they can be simplistic, overused, or embraced too fiercely by some trainers. In reviewing my classes at The Ranch and my various seminars, however, I discovered that there are a few sayings that I do share with my students regularly. It made me wonder why these statements have stuck with me over the years, and I thought I'd share why I find them so helpful when I teach. I don't usually quote the saying verbatim, but I always give credit to the trainer who made the concept resonate for me. Here are some of my favorites:

1. "I'd like to share my biases" —Kathy Sdao

I heard Kathy make this statement in the introduction to one of the first lectures I saw her present. She explained that while she tries her best to be objective and factual, she recognizes that she brings biases from her own experiences and background to the podium when she lectures. She then described those biases. I now use a similar approach, because I think it is helpful for the listener to know that I can't help but look at a topic through the filter of my own experiences. By sharing my training background and philosophy at the beginning of a lecture, I help my students better understand my point of view.

2. "Training is a mechanical skill" —Bob Bailey

I used to bristle at this statement because I felt that it diminished the importance of the skills we develop as trainers. As I gained experience and began teaching young trainers myself, though, I've learned the value of Bob Bailey's observation. So much of good training comes from precise clicker use, treat delivery, and observational skills. When these skills are practiced regularly, with care and accuracy, they become automatic and allow trainers to focus on other aspects of the behavior being trained. I equate the initial-skills acquisition to how I felt when I first learned to drive a car; at first, I had to really focus to stay in my lane and to respond quickly to brake lights in front of me, but with experience these mechanical skills became second nature and allowed me to concentrate on other aspects of driving, such as navigating. Today, I spend a great deal of time on mechanical skills with new trainers and appreciate the wisdom of Bob's assertion.

3. "The animals are the easy part" —Bob Bailey

I hear people quote this saying all the time, joking about how difficult clients can be. While I agree that the "people part" is often more difficult than the "animal part," both are crucial for the success of training, and both involve similar training abilities. I prefer not to dwell on "what's wrong with our clients," but rather explore how to get the client to a level of proficiency and understanding necessary for success. Some of the best trainers I know fail as consultants because of their lack of people skills; I believe it is important for our community to make the use of positive reinforcement with people a priority when we teach people how to train.

4. "Unlabel me" —Susan Friedman

Susan encourages us to be careful with the labels that we put on animals: he's phobic, she's frustrated, he's temperamental. This idea goes to the heart of what we should be doing as trainers when we solve problems. Too often we put a label on a behavior and assume that it explains the behavior or the cause of a problem. Susan's saying reminds us to go further than simply calling an animal "aggressive," for example, and instead describe what the behavior looks like. Is there data about the frequency, context, consequences, and other factors that can help us train more effectively? It's okay to use terms such as "aggressive" or "playful" as long as we remember that they are just convenient labels, but we must describe the behavior and its context clearly if we hope to be successful at changing that behavior.

5. "The only thing two trainers can agree on is what a third trainer is doing wrong" —Steve White

When Steve uses this line, he always gets a laugh. The humor lies in the truth behind the statement. As a community of trainers, we can be very opinionated and critical of one another. I see this saying as a call to action: we need to be more open-minded and welcoming of trainers who train differently. Our training communities are becoming more and more closed-minded and less accepting of outside thoughts. We will be more successful spreading our positive reinforcement strategies and ultimately help the animals we care for better if we approach each other with kindness and understanding and use positive reinforcement with one another.

6. "It's just behavior" —Karen Pryor

I have seen Karen reassure skilled trainers who are dealing with complex behavior problems by saying, "It's just behavior, and you know how to shape behavior!" In these instances, Karen was not trying to minimize the seriousness of the behavioral problem. She was reminding trainers that no matter how challenging an issue, returning to the basics will help find solutions to the most difficult behavioral situations. I think of this statement every time I take on a complex consulting job that concerns me; I remind myself to look at the environment (antecedent arrangements and consequences) and break the problem into its smallest component parts. When I remember that it's just behavior, suddenly the problem doesn't seem quite as overwhelming!

7. "The rat is always right" —B.F. Skinner

B.F. Skinner's famous phrase and its derivatives—"The animal is always right," "The dog is never wrong," and so on—remind us that animals behave the way they do based on past experiences in particular contexts. If you want to change an animal's behavior, you need to change what you are doing. Trainers must accept responsibility for getting desired behavior from animals. In scent-detection work, we use a corollary idea: "Trust your dog." Once you are in the field, if you have trained the dog well, if the dog indicates that he has found something, believe him!

8. "Training is not a luxury" —Ken Ramirez

Please indulge me while I share one of my own sayings, which I use in every class and seminar that I teach: Training should not be considered a luxury but should be a key component of any good animal-care program. Behavior management, which includes training and enrichment, ought to be a cornerstone of good animal care alongside veterinary care, nutrition, a proper environment, and appropriate social structure. In many animal-care programs, training is an afterthought, something to do if there is time. Elevating the importance of training in the minds of the public and in the minds of animal-care professionals is one of my ongoing life missions.

I am sure there are other sayings that I use from time to time, but these are the most relevant and useful to my teaching. I am grateful to the many trainers who continue to be my teachers and provide valuable mental models.

Recognizing New Criteria

In Karen Pryor's original "Ten Laws of Shaping," she encouraged trainers to relax old criteria when they are introducing new criteria. Trainers sometimes fail to recognize new criteria, which is one of the reasons Karen adjusted the wording of her "laws" in her 2014 update, "The Modern Principles of Shaping" (see next page). Her revised wording suggests that trainers should "relax old criteria when something changes." This might seem like a minor and insignificant change, but I think it helps less experienced trainers recognize the need to lower criteria in a wider range of circumstances. I want to revisit this simple guideline because frequently I find myself suggesting that trainers lower their criteria.

For example...

A trainer moves a dog into a new room in the house and the trainer's expectation is that the dog should respond perfectly, even if that behavior has never been requested in that room previously. I point out that the criteria changed, something is different to the dog, and it might be helpful to lower criteria. Experienced animals will learn to generalize to new surroundings and, with experience, may be able to perform to original criteria in any setting. But when that fails to happen, I recommend listening to the dog; he is indicating to you that something is different.

A similar problem arises when an animal is expected to share his trainer with another animal for the first time. Even if both animals perform perfectly when they are alone and know each other well, if being worked as a pair is new to them, that is new criteria. Working together is a significant change from both animals' perspectives. It should not surprise the trainer if some well-trained behaviors deteriorate under those circumstances.

Even what appear to be insignificant changes—a new plant in the corner, a new paint job on the walls, the furniture recently rearranged, working at 2:00 a.m. for the first time, or introducing a new type of treat—can have an impact on behavior. Be forgiving when your animal indicates that he is uncomfortable with a change.

I hope these examples expand trainers' understanding of "new criteria." When previously reliable behavior starts to deteriorate, it is usually an indication that there is something different in the environment. Ideally, trainers should recognize that there is something different and be prepared to adjust criteria before things go wrong.

The Modern Principles of Shaping

by Karen Pryor

1. *Be prepared before you start.* Be ready to click/treat immediately when the training session begins. When shaping a new behavior, be ready to capture the very first tiny inclination the animal gives you toward your goal behavior. This is especially true when working with a prop such as a target stick or a mat on the ground.
2. *Ensure success at each step.* Break behavior down into small enough pieces that the learner always has a realistic chance to earn a reinforcer.
3. *Train one criterion at a time.* Shaping for two criteria or aspects of a behavior simultaneously can be very confusing. One click should not mean two different criteria.
4. *Relax criteria when something changes.* When introducing a new criterion or aspect of the skill, temporarily relax the old criteria for previously mastered skills.
5. *If one door closes, find another.* If a particular shaping procedure is not progressing, try another way.
6. *Keep training sessions continuous.* The animal should be continuously engaged in the learning process throughout the session. He should be working the entire time, except for the moment he's consuming/enjoying his reinforcer. This also means keeping a high rate of reinforcement.
7. *Go back to kindergarten, if necessary.* If a behavior deteriorates, quickly revisit the last successful approximation or two so that the animal can easily earn reinforcers.
8. *Keep your attention on your learner.* Interrupting a training session gratuitously by taking a phone call, chatting, or doing something else that can wait often causes learners to lose momentum and get

frustrated by the lack of information. If you need to take a break, give the animal a "goodbye present," such as a small handful of treats.

9. *Stay ahead of your learner.* Be prepared to "skip ahead" in your shaping plan if your learner makes a sudden leap.
10. *Quit while you're ahead.* End each session with something the learner finds reinforcing. If possible, end a session on a strong behavioral response, but, at any rate, try to end with your learner still eager to go on.

Misconceptions about Shaping

In 1999, Paul Chance defined shaping as "the use of successive approximations to achieve a target behavioral goal." In 2017, David Pierce and Carl Cheney used an almost identical definition, adding only that shaping includes the use of "selective reinforcement." Based on those definitions, most of us use shaping every time we train. Yet, trainers still have misconceptions about shaping, and I find myself having to address those misconceptions with my students and clients. Here are five of the most common misunderstandings.

Misconception 1: Targeting is not a form of shaping.

This is one of the most common misperceptions I encounter. When you use a target or any type of prompt, you are still relying on successive approximations and using selective reinforcement to achieve the goal behavior. Target training is shaping, or "shaping with a prompt."

Misconception 2: Shaping and free shaping are the same thing.

The term "free shaping" does not appear in scientific literature. It is a relatively new term that refers to the type of shaping where the trainer uses no deliberate prompts and makes no conscious attempt to adapt the learning environment to make the desired behavior more likely. Instead, the trainer captures small movements offered by the animal and gradually makes approximations toward a desired goal. Many people think of free shaping as "shaping," and hence that any arrangement of the environment is not "real shaping." This perspective may stem from Skinner's original work with animals in an operant chamber where there was no obvious trainer interaction with the animal. The belief that shaping must be free of prompts in order to be "true" shaping is the cause of so much confusion.

Misconception 3: Free shaping does not rely on arrangement of the environment to achieve results.

All behavior is impacted by the environment. Even if the trainer does nothing consciously, the environment influences the animal's learning. By bringing the dog to a room, closing the door, and sitting near the dog with a pouch full of treats, the trainer relies on some environmental arrangement. Moreover, setting up the environment is an essential way to help an animal succeed, and it is a mark of good training. For example, placing a toy or a prop between you and the animal may encourage the animal to interact with the object; it is a good way to start a free-shaping session.

Misconception 4: Free shaping is a better way to train.

I do not consider free shaping to be a better way to train. Free shaping is a difficult skill to master, particularly for novice trainers who can frustrate the animal easily. Professional trainers need to know how to free shape, but they should prioritize using whichever technique is going to set up the animal for success the best.

Some trainers prefer to train without prompts so that the animal figures out the behavior on its own and is not dependent on external environmental cues. However, the animal will still perceive environmental cues while training. That is why some dogs have difficulty transferring behavior into new locations or new contexts; all the new environmental cues in the new location were not part of the initial training. If you don't focus on the environment in the beginning, you will need to focus on it eventually.

Whether a trainer uses capturing, targeting, luring, molding, or free shaping, every technique has benefits and drawbacks. Skilled trainers will know how and when to use each one.

Misconception 5: Mixing free shaping with other techniques is wrong.

There is nothing wrong with combining techniques. People believe that certain techniques must be used in their "purest" form because some professional dog training schools and programs, including the Karen Pryor Academy Dog Trainer Professional program, require their students to learn how to shape behavior with minimal to no prompting. These professional dog training programs teach students to use all the available training tools, focusing on each tool separately, so that the student can use them in an expert manner when needed. A basketball coach may ask an athlete to practice passing, dribbling, and shooting free throws during certain segments of practice, not because the athlete will use *only one* of those tools in a game, but because it helps athletes develop each skill thoroughly before an actual game. Similarly, a trainer should practice and learn various individual techniques so that when s/he works with an animal, s/he can adapt and mix the techniques as needed.

Final thoughts

Sometimes we overcomplicate things in the training world. I don't think many trainers are purely free shapers; most of us use a variety of techniques, because our goal is to help animals succeed. There is no merit in suggesting that one technique should always be used; some techniques should be combined if it will help the learner.

The Many Faces of Targeting

After my concept training Lab at a recent ClickerExpo in Europe, one attendee approached me with a problem. She wanted to try an exercise that I had suggested that required her to use targeting and prompting, but she was concerned because she had been taught that "shaping is the only real way to train; using a target is sloppy and the sign of a weak trainer."

Trainers sometimes become more proficient at using certain training tools more than others. They can become so passionate about their preferred tools that they push the other tools aside or even claim that the other tools are unacceptable choices. Shaping is an excellent tool, but it is only one of the many ways to teach behavior. You can shape, capture, lure, target, mold, or set the environment up in ways that assist the learner in achieving a desired training goal.

In my work with concept training, I have used targeting as an indicator behavior as well as a method for teaching new behaviors quickly. I've used targeting in training medical behaviors to help an animal learn to work with new equipment and to participate in new procedures in just a few sessions. Having a full grasp of targeting principles lets a trainer teach new behaviors to an animal in one or two training sessions. For targeting to be a truly versatile tool, I like the animals I train to acquire a large targeting tool set. Here are the various ways in which I like to use targeting and the order in which I teach these skills:

Basic Targeting: The first targeting behavior I teach an animal is touching its nose to a hand or a buoy on the end of a stick. The object being touched is referred to as a target. This simple form of touching an object is the foundation for each of the other targeting skills.

Follow Targeting: The next natural step is to teach the animal to follow the presented object. I use a target to guide the animal from place to place, into a kennel, onto a scale, or through an obstacle course, for example.

Variety of Targets: Next, I teach the animal that the target can take on a variety of forms, colors, or textures. This instruction allows me to transfer the touching behavior to other objects—an X-ray plate, a harness, or any selected object. It is also useful if you can cue the behavior in ways other than presenting the object in front of the animal, such as pointing at the object or giving a verbal cue. In concept training, it is helpful if the animal can target any object when indicated.

Another creative type of targeting is using the light from a laser pointer as the indicator for what the animal is supposed to touch. You can use the light to indicate a particular target from a distance, especially with animals trained in protected contact.

Varied Body Parts: Once the animal has grasped some of the more basic forms of targeting, I like to teach the animal to touch different body parts to an object: a hip, the chin, the rear feet, or any other body part. This behavior has always been essential to my training, whether it is getting my dog to target her feet (stand) on a platform, putting her chin in my hand for eye drops, or targeting her head into a harness.

Extended Targeting: For some behaviors, especially medical behaviors, an animal may need to remain in contact with an object for extended periods of time. Extended targeting can be used for radiographs, ultrasound exams, nail clipping, applying a bandage, and many other procedures. I have always considered lying on a mat, sitting on a platform, and standing on a perch forms of extended targeting. Trimming a dog's nails can be handled more easily if the dog targets her paw to your hand for an extended period of time.

A to B Targeting: An animal can be taught to transfer its focus from one target to a new target. This type of targeting helps move the animal from one trainer to another or from one location to another.

Multiple Targets: Finally, an animal can be asked to touch two different targets, or two different body parts, at the same time. This is an advanced type of targeting and, in my experience, one of the most difficult types of targeting to teach. For example, it is challenging to guide a dog's back feet to one location and her front feet to another location. At The Ranch, I am training a mini-donkey to target her left side (hip and shoulder) against a fence in order to keep her stationary while, at the same time, training her to target her lower jaw to my hand so I can administer a deworming paste in her mouth.

The creative trainer can find other ways to put targeting to use. It is a helpful tool that I encourage trainers not to overlook. Targeting is more than simply touching an object or using an object to prompt a behavior. When trained correctly, targeting strategies can become a set of building blocks for developing many different behaviors.

Training by Any Other Name

Often, I find myself sharing my belief that training is not a luxury, but an integral part of a good, responsible, and professional animal-care program. I imagine that most professional trainers have clients, friends, and relatives who don't quite get training. They don't understand training and don't recognize its importance. In other cases, however, training takes place without people realizing that it is happening at all.

When I consult at zoos, keepers tell me that they don't train their animals, yet each animal comes to the back when called, or goes out to the public exhibit when cued. Sometimes, there are even more examples of good behavior-management that the keepers don't recognize as training. These examples range from the use of enrichment to specifying locations where the animals wait to be fed. As a result, I spend a good portion of my consult explaining that the animals are learning, and that the keepers are already involved in basic training. My explanations are always intended to help them expand and improve their programs.

Pet owners can have similar beliefs. Clients tell me that they love their dogs, but the dogs are too dumb to train. Despite this assertion, each dog knows exactly when it is time to go for a walk, can predict when his mom is leaving for work, or hides in the basement when scary Uncle John comes to visit. I explain to clients on a regular basis that their dogs are far from dumb, and are, in fact, very trainable—look at all they have learned!

Good donkey or trained donkey?

In the summer of 2017, I was busily preparing for the arrival of the first animals at The Ranch. I visited rescue centers and breeders, looking for the perfect residents for The Ranch. Recently, we acquired nine wonderful mini-donkeys, ranging in age from two to eleven years old.

The mini-donkeys were brought to The Ranch by a couple, Sally and Leon, who had raised the donkeys since birth. I spent time with the couple at their farm and admired how much they loved their donkeys. At one point, I asked how much time they spent training the donkeys. Sally's response was, "Oh, we don't train them at all." As she said that, she called one of the donkeys by name, and it trotted over to her. Sally then picked up a harness and showed it to the donkey; the donkey stuck her head into the harness immediately and allowed it to be clipped on.

I commented, "They seem well-trained to me." To which Sally replied, "Nah, she's just a good girl; she's well-behaved."

I nodded and smiled and watched her interact with the donkeys. She loved them, and they clearly loved her. As my visit continued, I witnessed many more examples of how "well-behaved" the donkeys were. When Sally showed them a brush, each donkey positioned itself to be brushed. "They love having their coats brushed," Sally said.

Later, we were out in one of the barns where Sally and Leon had created a special stall with brushes attached to one side—so that the donkeys could brush themselves whenever they wanted. There was a small opening in the fence, created so that baby donkeys could get away from the older donkeys if they were being bothered. The whole set-up was thoughtful and enriching.

I never insisted to Sally and Leon that they were training their donkeys. It didn't seem important to convince them that they were actually good trainers. Sally and Leon were giving their animals a great life. They were putting the needs of the animals first. In their minds, they were just doing what needed to be done to give the animals a happy and fulfilling life. Isn't that what really matters?

I wish all of the people who interact with animals were that caring, that thoughtful, that in tune with their animals' needs. For some people, like Sally and Leon, good training comes naturally. When you care about your animals, are responsive to their needs, and listen to what they tell you, you end up shaping desired behavior. Training, by any other name, is still good for the animal.

Foundation Behaviors: A Practical Perspective

I am regularly asked, "What are the first behaviors that we should train our animals? Does the order matter? How do we determine what to train first?"

It depends!

No two animals are exactly alike, and no two training situations are exactly alike, so my initial response to the question of what to train first is always, "It depends!" However, I do use a specific sequence when I train a new animal, and I will share it with you here.

1. Approach and eat

If an animal does not willingly approach and eat from me, I cannot start training. While this may seem obvious, I regularly encounter trainers who fail to recognize this fact (see "Tiger Trust," p. 66). Before doing any type of formal training, it is important to teach an animal to approach you and take food from you. The only exception might be a remote training project that does not involve the animal and trainer having any interaction with each other, but, even then, it is impossible to shape behavior until the animal approaches and accepts reinforcers. My priority is always the animal's well-being, welfare, and comfort, and I work to create an environment that is comfortable and safe.

2. Follow

After the animal approaches and eats from me, I teach "follow." I continue to feed, and gradually work until the animal follows me when I take a step to the right or left and stays with me as I back away several steps, which indicates increased comfort and trust and is a sign that the animal is ready for more formal training.

3. Target

Next, I present a target: a hand target or a physical target, depending on the animal. Some animals are curious and sniff, investigate, or touch new objects presented to them—with those animals targeting is easy. For animals that are cautious, or less likely to touch a target on their own, I proceed more slowly. I work toward targeting because I find targeting to be an important building block for so many future behaviors (see "The Many Faces of Targeting," p. 25). Once an animal is targeting readily, I know that I have developed a level of comfort and trust and we are ready to proceed.

4. Clicker

Now I am ready to add a clicker to my targeting. Only once the animal is comfortable and is approaching, taking food, and targeting with me reliably do I introduce the clicker. This surprises some trainers who are accustomed to using a clicker from the very first interaction with an animal. The idea of using the clicker from the start probably developed from the introduction of clicker training to pet owners who already have a great relationship with their pets. When you start with an animal that already knows, trusts, and takes food from his trainer, it makes sense to use a clicker from the beginning. When a clicker is used too soon with animals that do not trust their trainers, however, the click is likely to be associated with scary experiences, and the click does not take on the desired positive properties.

I have worked with exotic animals, farm animals without a training history, and animals in shelters whose past interactions with people have been less than ideal. I have seen well-intentioned trainers start clicking with an animal that is still fearful, not eating, or poised to flee. It is important to save the clicker until the animal is completely comfortable in his environment. Waiting until the animal reaches that comfort level allows the click to develop the strongest possible positive reinforcement value. In some cases, I do not use a clicker at all, especially if the noise itself is scary to the animal. In those environments, I may use a different marker such as a soft whistle or a word.

5. Station

I like to establish some type of default stationing behavior. A default stationing behavior is a behavior an animal does or a place that an animal goes to while waiting for the next cue, when the animal is anticipating reinforcement, or whenever he is in doubt about what to do next. Stationing can come in many forms: a sit behavior, eye contact, going to a mat, jumping onto a platform, or moving into a heel position. In some cases, I look to establish a station before targeting because it gives the animal a comfortable place to be, a location or behavior that will always get reinforced. Actually, as soon as the animal starts eating from me, I start to create a station, but it is at this point in the training process that I focus on stationing as a formal defined behavior.

6. Follow target

I introduce the idea of following a target to any location and to varying distances early in an animal's training journey. When the concept of following a target is well established, I use "follow target" to guide an animal into doing hundreds of behaviors: kenneling, scent-detection indications, medical behaviors, research projects, guide-dog work, service-animal skills, agility behaviors, trick training, and so many more.

7. Tactile

Tactile interaction is a foundation to training many desirable behaviors. With time, the animals I work with often seek out and enjoy being touched. But at the beginning, I think of tactile as a behavior, and I approximate touch gradually. I pay close attention to the animal's body language and only touch when the animal truly allows it; I don't progress if the animal shows any sign of shying away. I frequently use targeting as a great first step that leads to touch. In most cases, I avoid touching an animal's head and feet at first, as those can be very vulnerable areas. I usually start with the rump, side, and shoulders.

8. Management and husbandry behaviors

Once I have taught the foundational basics described above, I train management and husbandry behaviors. Management and husbandry behaviors include wearing a muzzle, wearing a harness, responding to a recall, riding in a car, standing on a scale, most medical behaviors—in short, anything needed for proper day-to-day care. These kinds of behaviors are needed throughout an animal's life and are a permanent part of my training plans at all stages of an animal's life.

Management and husbandry behaviors are important and should be trained as soon as the foundations are established. Sometimes, I am forced to use management and husbandry behaviors before they are ready or trained at all (for example, daily medication, immediate shearing and hoof trims necessary for health, moving and transporting animals). However, when it is at all possible to wait, I do. Management and husbandry behaviors benefit from already having a strong relationship and well-established foundation skills.

9. Capturing

Until this point, I have guided or directed the animal in his learning. Next, I teach the animal that he can make the click happen through behavior that he initiates. By this point, the animal has learned a few rules about training, including the need to go to a station or a default behavior. So a capturing session requires a different environmental set-up in order to teach the animal that a "new training game" and a new set of rules are in effect.

I make the environment totally different from a normal session. For example, instead of a side pouch, I hide treats somewhere that I can get to quickly. I try not to make this new stage look like a training session. I make sure there is no place to go to station, and I put some unique prop in the middle of the room. The animal will usually check out the prop, and I click and reinforce his initiative (in capturing sessions, I usually toss the reinforcer on the floor). The first capturing session is the most difficult one because the animal must initiate the action with no guidance from me other than a click. Sometimes I need to move around the room, so that the object is between me and the animal, until the animal discovers that he must initiate the behavior.

I continue to differentiate future capturing sessions from other sessions by setting up the room and the environment in a unique way. For example, with my dogs, I put an object in the middle of the room, leave the room, and sit in the doorway with a baby gate or doggy door separating me from the room where the dog is located. The set-up does not look like any other type of training session. I can see what the dog is doing, but he cannot get to me, and that encourages him to investigate the item. After about three of these sessions, I find that most animals recognize the new rules of this set-up, and I have a new way to train behavior.

I usually do one "capturing" session out of every four training sessions at the start. Once the animal learns to generate behavior in a capturing session, I then adapt that behavior through small approximations and shape it toward a new variation of the original behavior (this is sometimes referred to as free shaping). I go back to targeting sessions frequently because, initially, I can shape behaviors more quickly with a target. But once the animal has learned to offer behaviors in a capturing session, I want the animal to be comfortable moving back and forth between targeting and capturing.

Suggestions, not a recipe

These steps make up my plan for starting training with a new learner. This step-by-step plan has been very effective for me in my career, but it is just a starting point. It is my standard plan when I am teaching new trainers how to train, but it is not meant as a rigid set of rules or as a recipe that should be followed blindly. Training is not always linear; as an animal develops skills, I often train more than one thing at a time or move on to the next behavior while I am still strengthening previously learned behaviors. For example, I might teach a dog extended duration with a tactile behavior, introduce a muzzle, and try capturing a spin behavior all in the same day. It's essential to know how to watch animals and how to assess their comfort and adapt to their feedback and needs.

I share this foundation training plan as food for thought and as an alternative approach for getting animals off to the best possible start. Training is such an important part of developing relationships with the animals in our lives. It is important to start that relationship in the clearest possible way.

2

Should I Use That? Tools and Techniques

One of the most common requests I receive when I teach and consult is to answer questions about the science and the practical application of certain tools and techniques. Some of these tools—like the jackpot, the keep-going signal (KGS), or the end-of-session signal (ESS)—are not found in the scientific literature, so I explore popular literature and offer my perspective about them. Since there are also misconceptions about common and "well-understood" topics, such as clicker use and reinforcement, I discuss these concepts and tools to define them and their appropriate use more clearly and completely.

Is a Clicker Necessary?

Should we stop using a clicker? Do we really need it? A recent study by Chiandetti et al. has raised many questions about the efficacy of the clicker. The study, titled "Can clicker training facilitate conditioning in dogs?" looks at the differences among the use of a clicker, the use of a word as a marker, and the absence of a deliberate marker altogether. Under the specific set-up used in the study, the researchers found no pronounced difference among the three conditions. The authors did not suggest that people stop using a clicker in training. They were careful to point out the limitations in their study and encouraged readers not to jump to conclusions. Yet, that's exactly what many people have done. Those who don't like to use a clicker point to the study as proof that a clicker is irrelevant, while those who use clickers take offense, cry foul, and claim research bias. However, most of the questions that I have heard are raised by individuals who have not read the original research paper and only heard about the study through third-party descriptions.

My thoughts

I think it is important to recognize that studies of this type ask very specific questions that determine how the study is conducted, and the results need to be interpreted with great care. After reading the article, I am not surprised by the authors' findings. The dogs in the study were trained to push open a breadbox. After training the initial behavior through shaping, the researchers attempted to look at whether the clicker followed by food, a verbal marker followed by food, or a food reinforcer alone affected the dog's ability to generalize the learned behavior under two new conditions. One condition was labeled simple, a slightly modified breadbox; the second condition, which they labeled complex, required the same motor skills from the dog, but the apparatus was completely different.

The researchers concluded that there were no important differences in how well the dogs generalized to the new apparatus, whether the trainer used a clicker, a verbal marker, or the food-only reinforcer. I think it is important to point out, however, that the task was reasonably straightforward, and the trainers were able to deliver the reinforcer immediately after the task was completed. Often, the value of the marker is more pronounced with complex behaviors where precision is a key. The real purpose of the marker is to provide contiguity, an immediate connection between the behavior and the food reinforcer. Because the researchers were careful to make sure reinforcement was available immediately, which is good training, the need for a marker was less critical.

Most important, this study was not focused on the speed of acquisition of the initial task, opening the breadbox, just on the speed of generalization after the dogs learned the initial behavior. The study's data did show that the dogs trained with the clicker acquired the initial task in fewer attempts and in a shorter time frame than the other dogs. Additionally, the dogs trained with the verbal marker learned the initial task faster than those trained with just the reinforcer. The data indicate an average of approximately 80 attempts (12 minutes) for the clicker trained dogs, 110 attempts (21 minutes) for those trained with a verbal marker, and 125 attempts (27 minutes) with food reinforcement only. However, once the study moved to its primary focus, generalization, the difference between conditions was less pronounced.

Different study = different results

One of my colleagues, Lindsay Wood Brown, conducted a study for her master's thesis work in 2006 titled "Clicker bridging stimulus efficacy." In that study, she asked a very different question and concluded that a clicker was more effective than a verbal marker. Lindsay's study involved shaping dogs to touch a target in the middle of a room. She showed that dogs trained with a clicker learned faster than those trained with a verbal marker.

Why such different results regarding the efficacy of the clicker? The results aren't really that different, because the studies asked different questions, used different testing methodologies, and defined efficacy differently. Both studies, from my perspective, were well-designed and carefully conducted. Neither makes sweeping generalizations about what the study proves, and both were careful not to overstate the importance of their results. The Italian study compared the efficacy of the clicker in teaching generalization while Lindsay's study looked at the speed of initial behavior acquisition.

But I also believe studies like these highlight the difficulty of conducting research in a controlled setting that accurately reflects real-world training; therefore, it is difficult to draw concrete conclusions from a single study. It is often those with strong opinions about the use of a marker who are quick to want to glorify one study or attack another. Personally, I think both studies have merit. They provide food for thought and allow me to ask further questions about what I can do to make my training better. I have not looked at or questioned whether a clicker is faster for teaching generalization. When teaching generalization, I tend to focus on other things such as fluency, gradual exposure to the new stimuli, and tools beyond shaping (the only teaching technique used in the two studies).

What neither study intended to clarify was the skill level or other tools needed to be a successful trainer. After all, the clicker is just one of many tools that can aid in shaping behavior. There is no magic in the clicker; it is just a toy noisemaker. The effectiveness comes from the way we use it combined with other tools. The click facilitates consistent, immediate communication. The accuracy of a clicker is based on our ability to observe behavior and react appropriately. Like most training tools, it requires skill to use effectively. I know Lindsay to be a skilled trainer, and I presume the Italian trainers were also skilled, but it was not a factor that was accounted for in their study, so it is impossible to evaluate that key factor based on the reported results.

Using a marker

So, back to my original question, is a clicker necessary? While it may not be necessary for learning to occur, a clicker is an excellent tool that, when used properly, can facilitate better training. Animals can and do learn without deliberate human-created markers; a marker may not be needed when reinforcement can be delivered immediately. Below are some general guidelines and thoughts about marker signals that I have shared in response to the many recent questions I have received.

Why I use a marker:

- A marker signal is useful in communicating the exact moment that an animal performs a behavior correctly.
- Animals find predictors of reinforcement in their environment; if you do not teach a marker, they will find a naturally occurring marker. Because of that fact, I like to be more deliberate and teach a specific marker that I can control.

- A marker is helpful for complex behaviors, when the trainer desires to reinforce a precise movement or action, or when the behavior is performed at a distance and immediate delivery of reinforcement is not possible.
- I like the precision and consistency of a mechanical marker, but verbal, visual, tactile, and other types of markers can be effective if used with care and precision under the right conditions.
- Markers assist me in the evaluation and coaching of young trainers, as a marker allows me to more clearly evaluate their timing—it is a useful teaching tool.

My guidelines for marker use:

- A marker is most effective when used while the correct behavior is still taking place, not after the behavior is complete.
- The best marker is one that the animal can perceive easily, is unique to the environment, can be replicated by all trainers easily, and has no previous negative association. For these reasons, the most effective marker will vary depending on the animal and the environment.
- The marker alone will not create stronger behavior; it must be timed right and paired with effective reinforcers.
- Good use of a marker requires practice. I prefer that trainers play training games and develop the motor skills to use a marker in practice before using it with an animal.

Continue asking questions, keep improving

Professional trainers need to be aware of all the tools that are available. Few tools are needed in every training situation, but good trainers understand the relative strengths and drawbacks of each tool. The best trainers will keep asking questions to better understand the techniques we use and to understand the science underlying each procedure. We do not need to have a knee-jerk reaction to studies where results differ from our own experience. It should simply prompt us to ask more questions. Are the study's findings scientifically sound? If so, why do they differ from my experience? Should I change my practices, adjust my understanding of the principles at work, or simply wait for more data and more information?

Whatever our response, we should remember that we are on a constant journey of learning and discovery. If we keep an open mind, our end goal should be to make our training and communication with animals clear and consistent. As practitioners, we should keep our eye on the science and keep up with new information, but we should never lose sight of our primary objective: the best animal care possible.

References:

Chiandetti, C. et al. (2016). Can clicker training facilitate conditioning in dogs? In *Applied Animal Behavior Science*,184, 109–116. Abstract at www.sciencedirect.com/science/article/abs/pii/S0168159116302386.

Wood, L. (2006). Clicker bridging stimulus efficacy. Master's thesis. Weblink at www.clickertraining.com/node/1960.

Ken's Top Tips for Reinforcement

I have many different guidelines and rules for using reinforcement effectively. But when I teach people about non-food reinforcers, more questions come up than usual.

I include the following tips to help trainers as they consider the possible explanations for the challenges they face. These are not all-inclusive rules. They are simply thoughts to keep in mind when training, points designed to guide you as you make your reinforcement strategies stronger.

1. *Don't take any reinforcer for granted.* There is no single reinforcer that will *always* be reinforcing. Remember that reinforcers are context-specific and may lose their effectiveness under certain conditions. As an example, kibble may be a great reinforcer for a dog in the confines of his home, but in the park it may not measure up to the reinforcement of the squirrels, other dogs, and new people in that environment. When you take reinforcers for granted, you are likely to be disappointed eventually.
2. *Understand the motivating factor behind each reinforcer and make sure to maintain its strength.* Each reinforcer has some aspect to it that makes it valuable to your animal. For the doggie treat it may be the smell or taste of bacon, for the tennis ball it may be the chance to chew it, and for the tug toy it might be the relationship and the play with you. If you fail to pay attention to the factors that make certain reinforcers motivating, you will see the reinforcement value of that item decrease—or, in some cases, disappear altogether. When you change treats, you may see the dog refuse the new treat immediately, or his enthusiasm may diminish. But sometimes it is not so obvious. What if the motivating factor of a tennis ball is the opportunity to chew it, but you throw it for the dog, asking that it be brought back immediately and assuming the reinforcer is chasing the ball? If you take the ball away too quickly, the dog never receives the value of the reinforcer: actually getting to chew the ball. If you are unaware of this subtle but important difference, the value of the tennis ball can decrease gradually over time. Always be aware of the factors that make each reinforcer effective, and work hard to maintain them.

3. *Evaluate the effectiveness of reinforcers constantly.* I ask myself regularly, "Is this reinforcer working?" If I am not able to determine the answer easily, I begin to set up a formal evaluation process to look at factors like "focus." I have always found that the level of an animal's focus is directly related to the power of the consequences being used in that training session. While there are many factors that impact whether or not a reinforcer is effective, I have discovered that by observing the animal's level and intensity of focus I can quickly determine if the reinforcers being offered have value. High-value reinforcers create razor-sharp focus, while low-value reinforcers create wandering eyes… and sometimes even wandering feet.
4. *Be aware of the expectations your animal has developed regarding reinforcement.* Depending on how and when you use certain reinforcers, animals will develop expectations about those reinforcers. If you always use a high-value treat for certain behaviors or are in the habit of giving a set number of treats in certain circumstances, your animal will come to anticipate and expect that level or value of reinforcement. You may find that if you change or lower the value of the reinforcer, the animal is disappointed. The animal may actually find the offered treat aversive because it did not match the expectations. If you want an animal to accept variety in the types of reinforcement you offer, that acceptance must be taught. I encourage the use of reinforcement variety early in every animal's training.
5. *Understand the value of access to reinforcement.* Always remember that if an animal has regular access to a reinforcer, its effectiveness may diminish. This goes hand-in-hand with understanding the motivating factors behind reinforcement, discussed above. I leave certain toys around for my dogs to play with when I am not home. Since some of the reinforcing value comes from the social interaction of playing with me, the toys are still effective reinforcers even though the dogs have access to them all day. However, if the primary value of the toys is chewing them, the toys may not have as much value if the dogs have had the chance to chew them all day long. Being aware of these possibilities can help you make sure that reinforcers have value when you are ready to use them.

6. *Look at behavior—the key to successful training.* Ultimately, it is most important to look at your animal's behavior to determine whether your use of reinforcement is successful. If you are seeing behavior that you like and want, your use of reinforcement is working. If you are not seeing desirable behavior, then something in your reinforcement plan needs to change.

The Jackpot Mystique: Tool or Trainer Superstition?

As I travel around the world lecturing about training, there are certain questions that come up again and again. The end-of-session signal, the keep-going signal, the least-reinforcing stimulus/scenario, and jackpots seem to create the most confusion. Perhaps this is because information about these concepts is not readily available in the scientific literature. These are tools that have come from the practical side of training and have been promoted by trainers who needed to make certain concepts clearer to their animals. As a result, there are no consistent or accepted definitions of these tools.

This article presents my definition of the term "jackpot," explores the use of jackpots and the mystique surrounding the tool, and discusses common mistakes with the use of jackpots. Finally, I share some suggestions for sorting through the information about a less-than-clear tool.

The fix-it fish

My first exposure to the use of a jackpot dates back many decades. As a young trainer working with dolphins in a small marine-life park in Texas, I used a variety of fish as reinforcers. One of the dolphins' favorite fish was mackerel, but, for a variety of nutritional reasons, each dolphin was only allowed one of those large fish each day. It was a highly valued reinforcer for the animals, and we reserved it for special breakthroughs in training. When one of us was training a new behavior, we would argue among ourselves to see who would get to use the fish for their sessions. When a behavior had problems meeting criteria, we reserved the fish for when the animal did particularly well meeting all criteria that day. We called this reinforcer the "fix-it" fish; the director of training told us that it was called a jackpot. As a young trainer, I remember marveling at the value of this magic reinforcer.

I remember clearly that the use of that fish both helped correct problem behavior and reinforce specific breakthroughs in new training. But is that memory clouded by the passage of time? Is it a fanciful myth that is perpetuated by our desire as trainers to have that elusive magic reinforcer? I am not certain. I have continued to use jackpots, albeit sparingly, in my training. But as I study and explore the science that underlies training, I keep facing the question: *Is the jackpot a unique tool, or is it just the use of good, well-timed reinforcement?*

Definition

Because the jackpot tool does not appear in scientific literature by name, trainers have taken the term jackpot—from its use in casinos, lotteries, and other games—and created their own unique definition. It could be argued that any definition of use of a jackpot as a behavior tool could be considered correct, since there is no resource to turn to for a consistent definition. For the purpose of this article, I would like to propose a definition that is a combination of definitions offered by Karen Pryor (1984; 2006), the zoological community (AZA, 2017), and my own discussions with and observations of professional trainers who seem to use the tool well.

A jackpot is an unexpected, high-value reinforcer used sparingly and contingently to reinforce a significant breakthrough in training.

Application challenges

Even if we can agree on a definition of a jackpot, that does not guarantee consistent application of the tool. In my experience I have seen several ways that the tool is used in detrimental or less-than-helpful ways.

The biggest challenges include the following:

1. *Drawn-out delivery:* When delivering reinforcement, I have seen many a trainer give the animal a dozen treats as a jackpot. But, instead of offering the treats all at once, he or she delivers the treats one at a time. By the time the last treat is offered, several seconds have passed, and it is doubtful that the later reinforcers are associated with the excellent behavior that the trainer intended to strengthen. The later reinforcers certainly reinforce the animal for good stationing or paying attention to the trainer. These results are not bad, but they are not the responses the trainer was intending to reinforce.

2. *Sloppy delivery:* Sometimes trainers toss a large handful of treats on the ground; as the treats scatter across the floor, the animal goes into a panic looking for all of the treats. Unless the animal has been trained to receive and enjoy reinforcement delivered in this manner,

this type of delivery may be aversive. This is particularly true if there are multiple animals in the room, and the form of delivery creates competition for the food.

3. *Overuse:* One of the supposed benefits of a jackpot is associated with the rarity of its use. Used too often, a jackpot creates an expectation on the part of the learner that large or high-value reinforcers for a particular behavior are common and, thus, expected. This assumption can cause lower-value reinforcers to be perceived as aversive. I am not opposed to the use of consistent high-value reinforcers for a critical behavior; I think that can be helpful. But I would not refer to that use as a jackpot.
4. *Scary novelty:* There are some who advocate that one of the advantages of jackpots is the novelty. However, I have seen trainers offer jackpots that were so novel that they frightened or confused the animal, and thus were counterproductive.
5. *Marker use:* There is a divide in opinions among those who use jackpots in training about the timing of its use. Some people deliver the jackpot immediately following the marker, which is the way I have used jackpots traditionally. Others claim that the effectiveness of the jackpot is dependent on it being delivered in place of the marker, a technique suggested by Karen Pryor (2006) and a technique that I have used in certain situations. This is clearly an area that needs further exploration.

Studying the jackpot

So far, the efforts to study the jackpot under controlled conditions have not proven very enlightening. One study that was conducted did not demonstrate that the jackpot is an effective tool (Muir and Rosales-Ruiz, 2009). However, that study did not use the definition or application of the jackpot that I have seen be most successful; the jackpot in the study referenced above was not used contingently on a significant breakthrough.

An area where there is a great deal of research is the area of conjugate reinforcement (Rapp, 2008). Conjugate reinforcement is the idea that one reinforces exceptional effort or increased intensity of a behavior with higher-value reinforcers than behavior at a lower intensity or level of strength. A process that has been identified and studied, conjugate reinforcement is the reason trainers find success in the use of high-value reinforcers.

Studies have also indicated, however, that variety in reinforcement value can create variability rather than reliability in learner responses. For behaviors that require greater intensity, such as pulling a cart, or increased recall speed, a high-value reinforcer seems to be effective in creating variability that allows the trainer to select and reinforce the desired increase in intensity. But, if the variability impacts the precision of a behavior, the high-value reinforcer has been more of a distraction, and perhaps it has even been detrimental. It is this anomaly that creates doubt that a jackpot truly has the desired impact on learning.

Until trainers begin collecting data and keeping good records on their uses of a jackpot, including a consistent measure of the way the jackpot affects behavior, any claims we make about its effectiveness are anecdotal. While I still use jackpots in my training, I wonder if I am simply applying a high-value reinforcer on some type of intermittent schedule. That question, combined with the fact that I change and adjust my application of reinforcement continually based on the learner's needs, means that it is difficult to be certain if any major improvement in the animal's performance is due to the jackpot alone or if it is due to a combination of factors, including the already-proven impact of conjugate reinforcers.

For example, I have often claimed that the excellent reliability of my animals' responses to the recall signal are due to my occasional use of jackpots for exceptional speed. This could be true. But there are so many other aspects to the training that are probably contributing to the success of the recall. The primary reason for the cue's success is likely due to my use of high-value reinforcers for all well-executed recall responses and a gradual increase in criteria for speed. I do give surprise or unexpected larger-value reinforcers when my animal shows exceptional response times, but is that just a superstitious behavior on my part? I cannot show data that indicate that an animal trained without those jackpots would be less reliable or slower, but, because of the importance of the recall and the success I have seen, I am hesitant to change my approach to training that behavior.

To use or not to use?

Based on my personal experiences, my own use of jackpots has never had a detrimental impact on my training. However, its benefits are still only conjecture, ideas based on successful results without supporting data to back it up. I am not going to throw the jackpot out of the toolbox, but I am going to take great care not to overstate its effectiveness—or even its existence as a real tool. For now, I will simply state that I am using high-value reinforcement contingently, and not give that practice a special name.

I hope that we can all begin to find a shared definition of the concept of a jackpot. I plan to look for ways to collect, measure, and interpret jackpot data, and I encourage others to do the same. Only then can we truly alleviate the confusion that surrounds this elusive tool.

References

AZA (2017). AZA animal training terms and descriptions. From AZA *Professional Development Courses*. www.aza.org.

Muir, K. and Rosales-Ruiz, J. (2009). The effects of jackpots on frequency of response and choice. Presented at *Association for Behavior Analysis Conference.*

Pryor, K. (1984). *Don't Shoot the Dog.*

Pryor, K. (2006). Jackpots: Hitting it Big. In: Letters from Karen. https://www.clickertraining.com/node/825.

Rapp, J. (2008). Conjugate reinforcement: a brief overview and suggestions for applications to the assessment of automatically reinforced behavior. In *Behavioral Interventions*, Wiley InterScience 23: 113-136.

The Confusing Keep-Going Signal

I am asked regularly about the Keep-Going Signal (KGS), a confusing training tool I first wrote about in 2009. The confusion about the KGS exists because of the varied uses of the term "keep-going signal" that appear in popular training literature. When I was researching my original 2009 article on the KGS, I found dozens of references to the tool being used in diverse scenarios, including with circus animals (Kelley, 1946), guide dogs (Landeman, 1971), search and rescue (Pryor, 1999), zoological training (Cover, 1991; 2002), and military applications (Bailey, 2007). While there were similarities between a few of the uses, the differences in some cases were striking.

Normally, we can turn to the scientific literature to help clarify terms, but there is no reference to a KGS in the currently available peer-reviewed journals. The KGS is a popular-use term, not a scientific one. Thus, trainers can define and use a KGS in almost any way they like; it would be hard to argue that they are wrong. In this article, I'd like to focus on the two most commonly used applications of the KGS.

KGS as a tertiary reinforcer

The most widely used version of the KGS is as a conditioned reinforcer, used to reinforce an animal partway through a long-duration task, such as a medical behavior, guide-dog work, or search-and-rescue efforts. When an animal is performing the desired behavior correctly, trainers use the KGS to indicate that the animal is meeting criteria and should keep going. If the KGS becomes a predictor of a marker signal (a secondary reinforcer), then, technically, the KGS is a tertiary reinforcer.

Tertiary reinforcers are defined in the literature as a type of conditioned reinforcer. The designation of "tertiary" is an indication of how many stimuli separate it from the primary reinforcer: a tertiary reinforcer is followed by a secondary reinforcer that is followed by a primary reinforcer (Bostow and Tompkins, 1999). A commonly used example of a tertiary reinforcer is a poker chip, because it is reinforced by money (a secondary reinforcer), which is reinforced by food, drink, or other human needs (a primary reinforcer).

There is a debate among skilled trainers about whether this type of KGS is necessary. Some suggest that when behaviors are properly trained to duration, a KGS is not needed. Others argue that if a KGS has been previously conditioned as a reinforcer, its use can speed up the training of duration behaviors. I have not found the need to use a KGS, but I have observed situations where it appears to accelerate training. Because I have seen it work, I am hesitant to discount it as a viable tool without further data.

KGS as a directional cue

The second common use of the KGS is as a cue to guide or direct animals from place to place—when an animal is trained to move in a specific direction as long as a tone (the KGS) is played, for example. When the trainer switches off the tone, the animal stops forward motion and begins changing its behavior (turning its head in various directions) until it hears the tone again. When the animal "finds" the tone, it moves forward again, in the direction it is facing when the tone resumes. This type of KGS is used in certain military applications to guide an animal from location to location, even when the animal has never been in those locations before.

This use of the KGS is as a sophisticated cueing tool that it is very different from the other type of KGS described above. Yet, it is clear why those who use it call it a Keep-Going Signal—it signals to the animal, quite literally, to keep going.

KGS as an unintentional development

At times, trainers condition a Keep-Going Signal inadvertently. Several years ago, I worked with a sea lion trainer, Missy, who was in the habit of talking to her animals throughout the training process. When Missy demonstrated one of her newly trained behaviors to me one day, the sea lion began performing the behavior, then suddenly looked confused and stopped before completing the task. Missy cued the behavior a second time, but again the sea lion started to exhibit the cued behavior only to lose enthusiasm and quit. It occurred to me that Missy was not talking to her animal as she usually did during her training. I suggested she try again, but this time she should talk to the sea lion as usual. Missy looked skeptical, but when she tried it, the sea lion completed the behavior without hesitation. Missy had unintentionally trained a KGS; the constant chatter had become an unintended part of the cue!

This example highlights one of the challenges of a KGS. Whether trained intentionally or by accident, the animal can become dependent on the KGS and fail to perform without it. The KGS becomes the cue for the last part of the behavior. When this occurs, the KGS is simply a prompt, and it carries with it the same challenges that prompts have: the behavior can become prompt-dependent, and the prompt itself provides no real value.

The future of the KGS

I have seen other uses of the KGS, but they all seem to fall into one of the two categories I just described—or into a combination of the two. To discuss the KGS, it is important to clearly define how it fits into the training process in order to have an intelligent and worthwhile discussion about its use.

There are references to the Keep-Going Signal in popular literature dating back more than 70 years, though it is used to describe entirely different procedures. The KGS is unlikely to disappear from the common vernacular, and trainers should be familiar with its alternate uses. I hope this piece has helped clarify the topic for you!

References

Bailey, Bob. (2007). "Marian & Keller Breland: Pioneers of Applied Animal Psychology," Supplemental presentation at *35th Annual Conference of the International Marine Animal Trainers' Association.*

Bostow, D. and Tompkins, B. (1999). *University of South Florida Behavior Analysis Glossary.*

Website: *http://www.coedu.usf.edu/abaglossary/main.asp.*

Cover, Kayce. (1991). *The Syn Alia Series on Animal Training, Volume 1: Bridge and Target Techniques Made Easy.* Syn Alia Animal Training Systems, Sarasota, FL.

Cover, Kayce. (2002). "Introducing the Intermediate Bridge," in *American Animal Trainer Magazine.* October, 2002.

Kelley, F. Beverly. (1946). "Prima Donnas of the Circus." Reprint from Liberty Magazine in *1946 Ring Bros. & Barnum & Bailey Circus Program.* Circus Lithographs, Sarasota, FL.

Landeman, Merril L. (1971). *Training Protocols: Instruction Manual for Guide Dog Trainers*. Institute for the Blind Publications, Bloomington, IN.

Pryor, Karen. (1999). *Don't Shoot the Dog*. Bantam Books, New York, NY.

Ramirez, Ken. (2009). "Keep Going Signals: Semantics, Myth, and Practice" in *Canis* (Scandinavian Dog Training Magazine), No. 2, 2009.

The End-of-Session Signal

Is the end-of-session signal beneficial or harmful? Should trainers use it or not? At the Penn Vet Working Dog Conference in 2016, I got into a debate with a group of search-and-rescue trainers about the end-of-session signal. It was a spirited discussion.

It's important to note that the "end–of-session" signal does not appear in the scientific literature. Rather, it is a practical device that emerged in the training community. Simply put, an end-of-session signal is intended to mean any deliberate, predictable cue that informs the animal that the training session is over. There is no consistent method of applying this tool, and a discussion of its merits and drawbacks depends on how it's being used.

Proponents

After a stressful or difficult work session, trainers sometimes give an animal an "all-done" signal. Trainers who do this explain that it serves as a reinforcer, signaling a break in the strenuous activity as well as an opportunity to rest.

Many working dogs, especially guide dogs and certain service dogs, are focused on specific tasks for lengthy periods of time. Trainers teach an "at-ease" signal that indicates to the animal that it no longer needs to be actively working until it is cued to re-engage. For example, when the handler and service dog arrive at a restaurant and the handler sits at a table, she will cue the dog to settle. This is sometimes considered an end-of-session signal.

Some trainers use an end-of-session signal because their dogs are so eager and attentive that they follow and watch the trainer after the session is over. Those trainers feel that an end-of-session signal gives clear information to their dogs; the signal means the dogs no longer need to pay attention and can do their own thing.

Opponents

Some trainers argue that an end-of-session signal is unnecessary, and even detrimental. If the signal means that the session is over, it usually indicates that positive reinforcement is no longer available. By definition, the removal of the opportunity for positive reinforcement is a time-out, which is technically a negative punisher. A time-out at the end of a session punishes the last behavior or series of behaviors.

So is it a good or bad tool?

Before those of you who use an end-of-session signal panic, worrying that you have been punishing your dog, relax—that may not be the case. Let's examine a few uses of an end-of-session signal and see how each has a different meaning to the animal.

Traditional trainers: Early in my career, before I learned about positive reinforcement, I worked in a traditional training program that used corrections. Under those circumstances, the end-of-session signal marked the end of stress and, thus, was probably a relief to the dog—serving as a negative reinforcer.

Guide dogs: In my work with guide dogs, we taught the dogs to "settle" when we didn't need them to actively guide their handler, as described above in the restaurant scenario. Many trainers refer to this "settle" cue as an end-of-session signal. But in my opinion, it's simply a relaxed "stay"—just another behavior in the long sequence of tasks asked of a guide dog. As such, it is quite beneficial.

Search-and-rescue dogs: In "When Training Is Too Much Fun" (p. 60), I write about Carson, a search-and-rescue dog that lost his alert behavior due to an inadvertent end-of-session signal. When the signal indicated, predictably, that it was time to go home, Carson was unintentionally punished. He enjoyed searching so much and was disappointed that the fun was ending.

This is what I think happens to trainers who use an "all-done" signal and always follow it by leaving for work or disappearing and leaving the dog alone. If a dog enjoys training, an end-of-session signal that is followed predictably by the trainer disappearing may be perceived as an unpleasant and punishing experience.

Positive alternatives: Some trainers use an "all-done" signal when they finish training, and immediately follow it with a variety of options. The "all-done" may be followed by an opportunity to go outside, the chance to play with a new toy, the delivery of a long-lasting chewy treat, or the start of cuddle time on the couch. In these instances, the "all-done" signal is not an end to reinforcement but is actually a cue to engage in a new reinforcing activity.

I used to work with a group of walruses, and at the conclusion of formal training we always provided them with clams, mussels, and other fun treats hidden in a mountain of ice. We cued the walruses when the opportunity to forage in the ice was available. Visiting trainers often thought it was an end-of-session signal, but we had trained it as a positive reinforcing cue.

Final thoughts

Because there is no prescribed way to use an end-of-session signal and its uses are varied, it's not possible to give the tool blanket praise or condemnation. Although the examples above may be referred to as end-of-session signals, that may be a misnomer. Each functions in a different way.

Many trainers use an end-of-session signal without knowing it: taking off the pouch, showing empty hands, walking away from the dog, or giving the dog a final short rub. All of these activities can become punishing if we are not careful.

The use or lack of use of a so-called end-of-session signal is not a barometer that indicates good or bad training. What matters is how the signal is being used and, most importantly, how the learner responds. The best use of the end-of-session signal is when it fades the trainer out of the situation. The removal of the person is not punishing previous behaviors but allows the reinforcement to run out naturally, as happens when the animal is cued to go play, or given a toy, or offered a treat puzzle.

Understand what you are reinforcing or punishing, and be poised to adjust what you are doing to make your dog successful. Observe your learner's behavior when a session has ended: if he is relaxed and comfortable and behaving appropriately, there may be no need to change how you end your sessions. If, on the other hand, you see nervous, frustrated, or problem behavior that coincides with the session ending, you may want to examine how you conclude your sessions. Observe what your animal is learning and doing, and listen to what his body language and behavior are telling you. Our goals should be to give clear guidance and to set up our learners for success.

3

Creative Solutions to Unusual Problems

So much of training is about problem-solving. All five of the articles in this chapter are stories that share a problem and the steps I took to try to resolve it. The subjects of the stories include, in order, a search-and-rescue dog that lost motivation after a few years; a sea lion that wouldn't work with new trainers; two tigers that became aggressive after their keepers implemented a training program; the introduction of two dogs when one had a history of serious aggression toward other dogs; and an alpaca that was shy and skittish.

When Training Is Too Much Fun

A few years ago, a search-and-rescue trainer named Sharon asked me to help solve a perplexing case. Her dog, an energetic five-year-old Lab mix named Carson, suddenly stopped alerting when he found a person during search trials. Sharon and Carson were a FEMA-certified team that successfully found and helped rescue dozens of people over a two-year period. Normally, Carson began his searches with great enthusiasm, running through the rubble, the field, or the specified search area, clearly on a mission. Sharon could tell when Carson found the scent of a person and was zeroing in on the exact location because his search pattern changed. He sniffed in a more focused way, and soon after alerted on a find, barking excitedly and looking directly at the location of the missing person.

At Carson's last real search, when Sharon knew he had acquired the scent and expected him to start barking, Carson kept circling a small area, sniffing and looking toward a fallen beam blocking a doorway, but never actually stopping to indicate. Sharon started calling out to see if anyone would respond, and she heard the faint yell of a person deep within the rubble. She called the rescue team, and a young man was carried out from the rubble safely.

Sharon pulled Carson from active duty temporarily. In retrospect, she had seen a decline in his enthusiasm for alerts on the previous three or four practice searches, though he still alerted successfully. She was concerned by the change in his behavior. After a veterinary visit, Carson was given a clean bill of health. He loved training and always seemed eager to go out on searches. At the start of all searches, whether they were practice or real, Carson began with enthusiasm and vigor, just as he had always done. "Searching for people" had been trained as a game, and it still seemed to be an activity he enjoyed. It was only the alert that was breaking down.

The cause of the breakdown was not immediately obvious to us. I asked whether Carson had been frightened by a victim on one of his recent searches. Lost or trapped individuals often are startled by the sudden appearance of a dog turning the corner, and they scream or yell, or even lash out and hit the dog. That type of reaction by the victim, understandably, can make the dog less eager to alert. I also worked with a dog that, for the first time in his life, found a dead body. The dog was not a human-remains search dog, and the find seemed to depress him and make his interest in searches diminish. Sharon assured me that none of these things had happened to Carson.

When a behavior breaks down, it either means that it's being punished inadvertently or that it's not being reinforced effectively. Sharon didn't feel that any of the punishers I asked about had occurred. Since there were no obvious aversives, we focused our attention on the reinforcers. After making a successful find and alert, Sharon played a vigorous game of tug with Carson. Sharon and Carson demonstrated the tug game, and it was clear from Carson's behavior that he enjoyed the game and found it reinforcing. Tug was a high-value reinforcer in other situations, and Carson seemed to enjoy the activity of searching. So why had the alert vanished?

I was reminded of a similar experience I had with highly motivated law-enforcement dogs. The dogs were so eager to search for the odor that they didn't want to quit. The search was so highly reinforcing that ending the game became aversive. As I shared that story, Sharon realized that this might be the problem for Carson. On her last four real searches, they were looking for a single lost victim. Immediately after the find, they played tug. Then, Sharon leashed Carson and put him in the car for the ride home. As much as Carson enjoyed the game of tug, it may have become an indicator that the searching game was over.

We began to retrain the behavior. We started each practice search with a two-minute game of tug, and then cued Carson to begin his search. When he found the hidden person, we rewarded him with more tug, and then cued him to search again for another hidden person. Within just a few repetitions of this game, we saw Carson's excitement for the alert return. The alert didn't necessarily mean the game was over! The alert always meant a fun game of tug. And tug, more often than not, meant there would be more opportunities to search. Within a few weeks, Carson's alert behavior was stronger than ever. Carson continued to work successfully for several more years. He and Sharon were responsible for finding and saving more than 100 lives—a very successful team!

Since that experience, I have seen similar scenarios occur over and over again, particularly in scent-detection work. The game of searching for scent is highly reinforcing for most dogs. A toy, game, or treat is needed to reinforce the alert behavior, but trainers must be careful not to make these toys predict the end of playing the sniff game. Otherwise, it can turn the toy, game, or treat into an aversive experience.

This story is a reminder that what we think is reinforcing may not be a reinforcer in all situations. We must be good observers of our learners' behavior. If we see increased enthusiasm and continued focus on a desired behavior, we know that our reinforcers are effective. When we see the behavior change and the interest or enthusiasm diminish, it means an aversive has entered the picture and, possibly, devalued the power of the previous reinforcer. We can never be complacent. Behavior is fluid and always evolving. We must remain vigilant to ensure that our animals are provided with clear and useful information.

Addendum

After the initial publication of this piece, the search-and-rescue (SAR) forums began to question the veracity of the statement "He [Carson] and Sharon were responsible for finding and saving more than 100 lives —a very successful team!"

Admittedly, this is an incredible number of finds, even for a very prolific search-and-rescue team. As a disaster search-and-rescue team, Sharon and Carson were often called to sites where many people might be trapped in a single search area. On one occasion, they were the first team to respond to a tornado-devastated building and they were able to make finds that each included dozens of trapped people. On that one day, they located three separate groups of people totaling 62 individuals. Similarly, Sharon and Carson were called in to several major disasters that included several days of searching; they found three to five people in each of those searches.

I hope this additional information puts the number "100" into context.

"I Don't Know You!" Dealing with Trainer Discrimination

Animals often exhibit various types of trainer discrimination. Some animals will work exceptionally well for certain trainers but want to bite others. When we are on the receiving end of an animal that snubs us, it can be an ego-deflating experience. Discrimination problems are usually the result of past experiences. They are often due to a lack of trust and indicate a need to work on building the relationship with an animal.

At the Shedd Aquarium, we acquired an older California sea lion named "CJ" from another facility. At the time, sea lions were new to our program, and I took an active part in CJ's acclimation and training. Although we had a staff of more than 20 trainers, there were 6 of us who worked with him regularly to maintain consistency while CJ got used to multiple people. He adapted to our program quickly, and we all loved working with him.

After three months, we began to introduce CJ to more trainers. He immediately began showing discrimination problems. If one of the six original trainers worked with him, CJ was excellent: he ate well and offered every behavior asked. If one of the new trainers tried to work with him, however, CJ quickly lost interest in the session. For a young trainer named Kelly, he seemed particularly stubborn. When she tried to engage CJ, he simply turned his head the other way. When she offered him a fish, he turned up his nose and refused to take it. When she offered fish inches from CJ's nose and asked for nothing other than the behavior of eating, CJ simply clenched his jaw tighter, closed his eyes, and turned his head away. Needless to say, it was a demoralizing experience for Kelly, who had several years of experience and was quite skilled and always kind to her animals. She had never experienced an animal responding to her in this way. CJ continued to respond with enthusiasm and energy to all of us with whom he had worked for the past three months.

We decided to take a unique approach to resolving this problem. Instead of simply exposing him to Kelly every day and waiting for him to get used to her, we wondered if we could teach CJ to accept new trainers through standard training approximations. Below is a training plan I wrote up for my sessions with CJ. We called this the Kelly Behavior, and I followed this plan step by step. (In parentheses, I have indicated how long we stayed at each step).

1. Treat sessions like normal; introduce Kelly as an observer or assistant (2 days).
2. Have Kelly touch CJ and do other tactile behaviors while I work and reinforce him (3 days).
3. Midway through a session, have Kelly step in and feed CJ one fish; I follow immediately by reinforcing him for eating the fish offered by Kelly (3 days).
4. Have Kelly offer a single fish at two or three different points in the session. Always follow with immediate reinforcement from me (4 days).
5. Have Kelly offer two consecutive fish once in the session and continue with Kelly offering single fish a few other times as in step 4 (3 days).
6. Recreate the above five steps with other trainers that CJ was already working with in my place (5 days)
7. Allow Kelly to step in and do a target, followed by a fish from Kelly, then reinforcement from me. Do this only once per session, but at unpredictable times during the session, while continuing with the progress described at step 5 (1 week).
8. Instead of targeting, try previous step with another behavior. Keep the behaviors simple and make sure they have a high reinforcement history (1 week).
9. Have Kelly ask for a single behavior two times during the session. Increase requests to three, then four times. Always follow a successful interaction with Kelly with heavy reinforcement from trusted trainer (2 weeks).
10. Have Kelly ask for two consecutive behaviors at one point during the session. Eventually increase to having Kelly ask for two consecutive behaviors three or four times in the session (1 week).

11. Increase asking for behaviors from two consecutive behaviors to three, four, five, then six consecutive behaviors (1 week).
12. Gradually increase the length of time Kelly works with CJ and vary that length of time frequently (2 weeks).
13. Increase from quarter to half to full sessions. Always follow with lots of reinforcement from a trusted trainer (1 week).
14. During steps 10–12, increase length of trusted trainers' absence; they should step around the corner out of sight for brief periods, returning for reinforcement (3 days).
15. Eventually, have Kelly begin a session without CJ seeing a trusted trainer in the area, with the trusted trainer only showing up after Kelly has worked with CJ for several minutes (5 days).
16. Intermittently, allow Kelly to do a complete session without a trusted trainer ever showing up (2 weeks).
17. Gradually increase the frequency of Kelly's solo sessions, until it is obvious that the trusted trainers' presence is not required to maintain CJ's attention and interest.

The plan worked! When we began this project, I did all the sessions with CJ and Kelly, but within a few weeks, all six of the original trainers could serve in the trusted trainer's role to help CJ get comfortable with Kelly. After three months, CJ and Kelly had developed a good working relationship, and the discrimination problem completely disappeared.

Relationships can be built with animals in many ways. At the start, our goal was just to train CJ to work with Kelly. What began as simply a behavior developed into a true relationship.

How did CJ respond to other new trainers? The next two trainers we introduced to him had the same challenge that Kelly had, at first. But we recreated our training steps and taught CJ to accept the new trainers in less than three weeks. After that, CJ accepted all new trainers without hesitation. He had learned that trainers in his new home could be trusted, and, while I am certain he recognized that new trainers were different, he no longer gave them any challenges.

Tiger Trust

When a training program is new, it can be easy to start down the wrong path accidentally, but if you can find a solution quickly enough, you can avoid serious behavioral problems. One such instance occurred when a zoo curator called me to help resolve a problem with two aggressive tigers.

The zoo's carnivore team had only been training their two full-grown Bengal tigers for a few weeks, but the trainers were convinced that the tigers "hated them." They explained to me that, at the start of every training session, the tigers displayed serious aggression. Before offering any advice, I asked to watch a session. The two keepers approached the enclosure with pouches of cut meat and long sticks designed to spear the tasty morsels that would be offered to the animals during the session.

The moment the keepers approached the holding area, both tigers charged straight at them and started hissing, growling, and pawing in the direction of the two keepers. Neither keeper reacted at all; it was obvious that they had seen this behavior before. Both keepers remained calm, and the expressions on their faces never changed. The tigers, on the other hand, were anything but calm. As the minutes passed, the tigers appeared to get more and more agitated. Finally, after what seemed like 10 minutes, the senior keeper looked at the other keeper and stated, "Let's take a time-out." The two trainers calmly turned around and left the area.

Immediately afterward, we met to discuss the session and the tigers' training history. The keepers explained that, from the start of the training program, the tigers had been aggressive and seemed to dislike the sessions. Before they implemented the training program, the keepers felt their relationship with the tigers had been great.

I asked, "How long have you been using a time-out like that?"

The keepers became defensive, stating, "We read that when an animal does something wrong, trainers should take a time-out! It's supposed to help..."

I quickly interrupted their protests. "I understand what you were doing; that wasn't my question. How long have you been using the time-out?"

"Since the beginning, four weeks ago," the youngest keeper explained.

I inquired, "In that four weeks, have you seen any change in the tigers' behavior?"

They thought about it a moment before the senior keeper said, "Oh, yes! It's gotten worse!"

That's what I expected them to say. "If I could get into the tigers' heads and anthropomorphize for a moment, as you two left the area, I think that the tigers were giving each other a high five and saying, 'Ha! We got rid of those keepers; we don't like them very much!'"

Unfortunately, using the time-out is an example of misapplying a tool—something that can easily happen to trainers new to the process. Time-outs are a type of punisher and, like any punisher, they can hurt a relationship, particularly when applied so early in the development of a training program. I reminded the tiger trainers that, although I would not recommend the use of a time-out, if it were going to work, it would have worked after the first few applications. All training tools, when applied properly, should show change relatively quickly. If they don't, the trainer must re-examine the application of the tool and make adjustments. I explained to the keepers that they had yet to develop a positive relationship with these two tigers, so the training sessions were not fun.

At first, the keepers disagreed, explaining that their relationship had been excellent before they began the training program. They were certain that, "Training is what ruined our relationship!" Since training normally helps to make a relationship stronger, I believed that the trainers had simply gotten the program off to a bad start. Perhaps they were expecting too much, or not setting clear expectations, or inadvertently had created a frustrating situation.

Over the next five days, we started over and began training as if it were a new concept. We did not concern ourselves too much with the aggression. In fact, the trainers simply walked into the area, tossed the tigers several big chunks of their food, and walked away. The tigers still growled and hissed, but the keepers were gone quickly, and the tigers seemed surprised to find food in front of them, which they devoured. The keepers returned and repeated the same procedure every 30 minutes throughout the day. Toward the end of the first day, the tigers quit growling when the keepers walked in; they waited expectantly for their keepers to toss the meat.

We continued with the same procedure on Day Two. The keepers were excited to see that not only had the tigers stopped growling and hissing, but they were quietly walking up to the keepers in anticipation of the food. This is what I was waiting for. Whenever we start to work with an animal that is shy, nervous, or frightened, the first behaviors we need to look for are approach and eat. We need to build trust. Until an animal is comfortable enough to approach the trainer and willing to eat in front of the trainer, continuing with a training session is pointless. Growling and hissing was the tigers' way of showing discomfort. When the keepers responded by withholding the food and walking away, it probably added to their discomfort and distrust. In less than two days, we had changed the tigers' behavior.

At the end of the second day, the keepers continued to come in and toss meat to the approaching tigers. But after tossing the meat, instead of leaving, the keepers stayed for a few seconds and tossed each tiger a second piece of meat, then walked away and left the area. On the third day, the keepers were able to increase the time between pieces of meat by several more seconds and even stayed long enough to offer a third piece of meat before walking out of the area.

By the middle of the fourth day, instead of tossing the meat into the enclosure, the keepers speared the meat on the end of a long stick, placed the end of the stick into the enclosure, and touched the ground with the meat. The tigers paused, surprised by the stick; one of them snarled and the other pawed at the stick and grabbed the meat. The keepers pulled their sticks out of the enclosure, tossed meat to each of the tigers, then walked away. That fourth day ended with the tigers taking meat off the sticks three times in a row before the keepers left. Best of all, as the keepers walked away, the tigers followed them as far as they could.

Trust was developing. By backing up, starting over, and setting clear, easy goals (approach and eat), we were able to accomplish more in four days than the team had accomplished in four weeks. Approach and eat progressed to approach and eat several pieces, then approach and eat several pieces from a stick, and, finally, approach and eat from a stick and follow the keeper. Day Five was even better; the keepers were able to progress to feeding as many as 10 pieces of food to each tiger in one session.

Although the keepers were eager to start training behaviors such as medical behaviors, they acknowledged they had made incredible progress and recognized the value of moving slowly. When the trainers built a strong positive reinforcement history, the tigers learned quickly that training sessions were a reinforcing experience, and the keepers began to re-establish the relationship they had lost. The keepers developed into excellent trainers; they simply needed someone to point them in the right direction. Today those two tigers are extremely well-trained and eagerly participate in every session.

We are all anxious to get to the "important" behaviors and to train "bigger and better" things, but there is no more important behavior than the foundational skill of eager participation by the animal.

Marlin Meets Tulip: A Systematic Introduction

In my years working in the zoological world, I have introduced aggressive animals to one another frequently. We moved animals from one zoo to another for breeding purposes, or to facilitate conservation projects. Some species, such as chimpanzees, tigers, and sea lions, can be quite aggressive when first introduced, and some species fight to the death instinctively. Over time, I developed a protocol for introducing potentially dangerous animals through a fence or barrier, working gradually toward safe, barrier-free interactions. I used this protocol to introduce two resident dogs to each other here at The Ranch.

Tulip

I brought Tulip, a Maremma sheepdog, to The Ranch to protect the livestock from predators. Tulip has a history of not getting along with other dogs, and she had attacked and injured her previous partner dogs. Livestock-guarding dogs usually work in pairs, but Tulip needed to find a home where she could work alone. Tulip adapted to life on The Ranch quickly and has done a great job protecting our alpacas, mini-donkeys, and goats.

Marlin

More recently, I brought Marlin to The Ranch from Chicago. Marlin is a bouncy, energetic, 8-year-old black Labrador retriever mix that I adopted from a Chicago shelter in 2013 to be part of an education program at the Shedd Aquarium. When the program ended in early 2018, I was eager to provide Marlin with a new permanent home. He made himself comfortable here at The Ranch immediately, enjoying the spacious pastures and a new life in the shadow of Mount Rainier.

The initial meeting

Tulip lives in the barn and spends her day with the animals that she protects. Marlin lives in the house. I planned to introduce them once Marlin settled into his new home, a few weeks later, but things didn't go according to plan! One day Marlin was on the back deck when Tulip saw him for the first time from the pasture. Tulip was a long distance away, but when she saw Marlin she launched into her protective-alert barking. This triggered defensive, reactive barking from Marlin, and the two charged at one another. Although they were separated by several fences and barriers, they ran toward each other and their barking became more aggressive and insistent. It happened quickly and unexpectedly; fortunately, I was able to get Marlin to follow me back into the house (hurray for recall training!). That initial incident lasted no more than 20 or 30 seconds, but it was not what I had hoped the dogs' first meeting would look like. Both had demonstrated serious aggression, and it did not bode well for future meetings.

Meeting on neutral ground

I made sure the two did not meet or see each other again without a plan in place. I decided to start by testing how they would react if they met on leash, from a distance, in a neutral place, away from The Ranch. Two weeks after the initial incident, my helper and I walked both dogs on leash at a nearby field, starting the session half a mile apart. I walked Marlin, my helper walked Tulip, and we reinforced the dogs with high-value treats. As long as we maintained a good distance, the dogs behaved; they saw each other but remained focused on the people walking them. The dogs' reactivity threshold was just under 100 yards; when we passed that point, both became agitated and began barking, growling, and pulling on their leashes. When we increased the distance between the dogs and passed the 100-yard mark, both dogs refocused on their respective trainers.

To introduce or not?

Did the two have to get along? Since one lives in the barn and the other in the house, the answer was not really. Given the unpredictable nature of life on The Ranch, however, I did not want to risk having them end up in the same space accidentally, especially considering Tulip's history of aggression.

I decided to use the introduction protocol I had developed working with exotic animals. I have used the protocol with dogs on several occasions, most notably on a project when we taught several seriously aggressive dogs to live together. It seemed an easy protocol to follow given the set-up of The Ranch.

Implementing the training plan

I was able to teach Tulip and Marlin to get along and share the same space after about six weeks of focused training. Here are the steps I followed:

1. *Work each dog in a separate pasture at the same time, providing them visual access to each other and starting just beyond their reactivity threshold.* I started this step with each dog as far away from the separation fence as possible, approximately 75 yards apart. Marlin was on the house lawn and Tulip in an adjoining pasture. They seemed unconcerned about each other and more interested in working with their trainers.
2. *Bring the dogs successively closer together until they can work on opposite sides of the fence without aggression or any signs of agitation.* This step took less time than anticipated. We moved 10 to 15 yards closer at each session and conducted three sessions each week. The dogs were able to work side by side on opposite sides of the fence by the end of two weeks.
3. *Let the dogs see each other regularly outside of sessions, but at a greater distance.* We continued training sessions across a shared fence line twice a week. When we were not in sessions, we gave the dogs daily visual access to each other, always with more than one fence or barrier between them. Marlin was in the lawn area while Tulip was two or more pastures away, at a distance of at least 30 yards, with clear visual access.
4. *Allow the dogs free time with a shared fence line outside of a session.* We continued twice-weekly training sessions opposite each other with the fence between the dogs and began to allow them supervised free access through the fence between sessions. At first, they ignored each other, but after eight days, the dogs became more curious, sniffing each other through the fence and chasing each other playfully along the fence line.
5. *Try brief, off-leash introductions in a neutral space.* After a week of calm interactions through the fence during free time, I decided to allow the dogs to interact without a fence in a neutral space, an enclosed lawn that neither dog sees nor uses regularly and, presumably, would be unlikely to want to resource-guard. That introduction went well (a more detailed description is provided below). Note

that we had been training with a shared fence line twice each week for a full month by this time.

6. *Move from a neutral space into one of the pastures for short periods of time, 20-30 minutes.* After the initial introduction in the neutral space went well for 5 minutes, I moved the dogs into one of the pastures to play.
7. *Gradually increase supervised pasture time.* These sessions went well (a more detailed description is provided below), and we continued them once or twice every week. The interactions continue to be peaceful and playful.

I tend to progress slowly when I deal with aggression and reactivity. I am conservative, because moving too quickly can trigger a reaction that can be dangerous and that can set back the training. After four weeks of training, however, I noticed that Tulip and Marlin were relaxed and showed no obvious signs of discomfort around each other when they had a fence between them. I moved cautiously but ended up progressing quickly because their behavior seemed to indicate that it was safe to do so. I always supervised and observed the dogs closely in case of trouble.

Tulip's and Marlin's social interactions

Tulip's and Marlin's reactions have become almost ritualized. They repeat the same sequence of behaviors each time they meet, just as they did the first time they were allowed off-leash together (step 5 above). As soon as they are brought into the same pasture, they run toward each other, sniff each other for at least 30 seconds, and then they bounce around playfully for another 30 seconds. After this greeting sequence, one of them takes off running with the other in quick pursuit. They run around for several minutes at top speed until one of the dogs disengages, and then they each proceed to sniff the ground and do their own thing for a short time. Tulip and Marlin seem to ignore each other and move to separate areas in the pasture for three to five minutes, and then one of them approaches the other and repeats the greeting ritual, followed again by the chasing game. On the occasions when I allow them to spend more than 20 minutes together, Tulip will reach a point where she goes into guardian-dog mode; she moves to the highest point in the pasture to lie down and survey the landscape. Marlin seems to take this behavior as a cue to leave Tulip alone and to sniff the pasture and explore on his own. I usually separate the dogs shortly after that. This interaction is good enough for my needs here at The Ranch.

Trained introductions, a useful tool

Although I did not originally design this program as an aggression-treatment protocol, I have used it successfully with hundreds of animals and have found that it reduces aggressive responses and increases compatibility. I often use the protocol even when I am introducing animals that have shown no aggressive tendencies, because I believe it creates a more comfortable introduction and reduces the likelihood of unexpected problems coming up later.

Why does the protocol work?

The dogs were counter-conditioned to each other's presence while being reinforced for calm cooperative behavior. I used multiple reinforcers during their training sessions: high-value treats, social interactions with favorite people, play, and mental stimulation. The dogs were desensitized to one another through gradual exposure.

Caution

Aggression-related training is never complete; social interactions are always changing and aggressive behavior, once learned, is not forgotten. I present this protocol hoping that others may find it useful in their training. Proceed with caution, since it may not be the right approach for every new animal introduction. With luck, it will be a valuable addition to your behavioral toolbox.

Salsa, the Untrainable Alpaca

I have always enjoyed alpacas and appreciated their gentle nature. About 16 months ago, I heard about a nearby alpaca ranch that had more than one thousand alpacas that were going to be slaughtered for meat later that week. I went to check the place out; I had no plans to adopt any alpacas that day, but I couldn't walk away without bringing home two. We named them Dulce and Roja. They were shy and skittish at first, probably because their only interactions with humans had been being chased and herded from place to place and occasionally being grabbed for shearing or a medical exam. I quickly became fond of these alpacas and felt that they would be happier with a few more companions.

Finding Salsa

A month later, I went back to the alpaca ranch hoping to bring home two or three more alpacas. Choosing from a herd with hundreds in each group was not easy. I selected an all-black female that I named Bandito and a large white female that I called Blanca. It broke my heart to watch the ranch foreman chase the animals around and man-handle them to put halters on them and prepare them for transport. I couldn't wait until I could provide them with a calmer, gentler home.

After I described my plans for the alpacas, the foreman scoffed, "Hah! These guys can't be trained; they're too wild. And the ones you're taking are the dumbest; that's why they were so easy to catch!" I didn't consider what I had just witnessed "easy." Twenty-five of the animals from the original herd had been separated and chased into a barn. The process of catching and haltering Bandito and Blanca took more than 45 minutes, and the animals remaining in the barn were frightened and huddled in a corner.

The foreman asked if I wanted any more before he let the remaining animals out of the barn. There was one spirited animal in the group that continued to pay close attention to everything we did, as opposed to simply fleeing. I decided that I had room for one more, and I pointed to her. The foreman said, "She seems awfully feisty; she might be too much of a handful." I said that was all right and she was the one for me. The foreman had great difficulty catching her. When he finally did get her, she spat a foul-smelling goop all over the foreman. It had a rank and spicy odor; at that moment I started calling her Salsa.

Social facilitation

Dulce and Roja welcomed Blanca, Bandito, and Salsa into the group, and they became a cohesive herd. I started their training by making their new home as comfortable and safe as possible: a warm shelter, plenty of pasture, non-stop access to hay and water, no more chasing and herding, no separations from the group, and easy opportunity to escape and avoid people if desired.

Salsa was comfortable with the group, and I attribute much of her later progress to social facilitation. Social facilitation refers to the impact on learning that an individual experiences in the presence of other conspecifics. For example, young animals will go through a gate or enter a kennel to stay with their mom. But when asked to do so alone, you may discover that they have not really learned the behavior—they were just staying with their mothers. With social facilitation, you cannot be certain the animal has learned anything specific, except to trust the group and stay with the group, but that facilitation proved helpful with Salsa. During the training, the other alpacas usually participated first, and their behavior encouraged Salsa's cooperation. Salsa was usually the last one to join in and the last to progress on each training step.

The training plan

Here is the training plan I used with the alpacas. It is based on my experience working with shy and skittish animals in a variety of settings over the years:

1. *Establish a comfortable environment.* Before progressing with more obvious training, it is important to increase the animals' comfort level and change their perceptions about people. I moved around the alpacas in smooth motions; I was never jerky or scary. I was careful never to chase or herd them. The alpacas always had a place to escape if they desired. The barn door was always open, and access to the outer pastures was always available. When anything startled the alpacas, Salsa was usually the first to run.

2. *Provide pellets in a predictable way in my presence.* I poured their favorite pellets (a grain-and-mineral feed designed for alpacas) into feeding troughs along the fence, then walked a great distance away to watch them eat. I reduced my distance gradually until I was able to observe them feeding while I stood only a foot or two away. Salsa was always my barometer for how close I could stand, since she remained the most cautious. It took several months of daily pellet-feeding for Salsa to accept me standing right next to the fence while she ate.
3. *Hand-feed browse from a distance through a barrier.* A favorite treat of the alpacas is browse, long branches full of leaves, that I affixed to the fence line regularly and that they seemed to love. I saved the longest branches, eight to ten feet long, and offered them to the alpacas by hand. I stood outside the enclosure against the fence holding a branch fully extended into the alpaca enclosure. The bravest alpacas, Dulce and Blanca, were the first to start eating the leaves from the end of the branches. Within a few weeks, they were working their way down the branch toward the fence and, thus, toward me. I made sure to move as little as possible. It took Salsa almost four weeks to start eating from the long branches that I held, and by that time the others were working their way toward me easily.
4. *Gradually shorten the length of branch.* Over time, I used branches that were only six feet long, then four feet long, then three feet, until eventually I only used one- to two-foot branches. At that point the alpacas were standing right in front of me with only a fence separating us. Even Salsa took leaves from these short branches.
5. *Offer pellets in long ladles.* Next, I wanted the alpacas to take pellets from my hand. I extended my arm over the fence while I was holding a long-handled ladle containing pellets. All of the alpacas, except Salsa, ate from the ladles the first time I tried it. Dulce and Blanca remained with me and ate well. The more nervous alpacas, Bandito and Roja, ate a few mouthfuls and retreated several feet away to chew the pellets at a distance. Salsa watched from a distance, and when Bandito and Roja retreated to eat she would spit at them! It

took Salsa only three sessions before she became daring enough to eat from the ladle.

6. *Gradually shorten the length of the handle until the cup is in my hand.* I took my time with this step. I chose to shorten the handle only when Salsa was ready, because I was seeing a benefit to progressing to each step as a group. Within six weeks, the alpacas were eating from the cup in my hand—no extended handle.

7. *Transition to inside the enclosure.* I moved inside the enclosure with my back against the fence, in the same place we had been training except that now there was no fence between me and the animals. I regressed to using the long-handled ladle and gradually shortened the handle just as before. This was a major step that took the alpacas several sessions to accept. Salsa needed almost a full extra week. Each time I took a significant step forward, it seemed to trigger Salsa's spitting—fortunately not at me, but almost always at Roja (Salsa and Roja tended to spend most of their time together outside of sessions). I had all five alpacas eating from the cup in my hand in under a month.

8. *Transition to feeding out of hand.* Once the animals were eating out of the cup with no hesitation, I transitioned to feeding directly from my hand. The alpacas definitely noticed the change, but their hesitation to eat from my hand lasted only a few minutes. At the end of the first session, all but Salsa were eating from my hand; she ate from my hand during the second session. At this point, my helper and I still carried the cups of pellets, but we were only allowing the alpacas to eat from our hands. The cups were strong cues that pellets were available.

9. *Move pellets to pouch.* After a few weeks of feeding from the hand, I moved the pellets to a pouch, and no longer brought the cups. This transition was relatively easy, and even Salsa did not seem to have a problem adjusting.

10. *Work one-on-one when possible.* Most of the work prior to this step was done by me alone or with the help of one other trainer. At this point, I

started to take advantage of the presence of students enrolled in courses at The Ranch, using them as training helpers. I coached the students through the steps and assigned an individual trainer to each alpaca. Each time I introduced a new class to the alpacas, we regressed to feeding out of cups and worked up to hand feeding by the end of the week. It took 12 rounds of students before Salsa was able to eat from the hand.

11. *Start touching lower jaw with fingers as alpacas eat.* As the alpacas' comfort level with feeding from my hand increased, I used the tips of the longer fingers on my feeding hand to rub the lower jaw of the alpacas. Predictably, Blanca and Dulce were the most accepting and Salsa was the least accepting.
12. *Begin using hand as target, mark, then feed.* I finally reached the point where I could present my hand and reinforce the alpacas for targeting. I considered using a clicker, but the sound was too loud and seemed to startle them, so I used a soft verbal "good." I was lucky to have Michele Pouliot, free-style champion and guide-dog training pioneer, coaching one of The Ranch classes at that time, so I asked her to help me work with Salsa. The targeting breakthrough occurred while Michele was working with Salsa.

Next steps

Today, Salsa is frequently the first to come to her trainer during training sessions. The alpacas are learning a variety of behaviors, including stepping on a scale, neck and head tactile, halter training, body tactile, and, eventually, foot and hoof tactile. Salsa is keeping up with the other alpacas, and in some cases has surpassed them. She still spits from time to time, but only at Roja (and accidentally at Roja's trainer), but those times are now rare.

It is often the animals labeled shy, difficult, skittish, stubborn, problematic, aggressive, reactive, etc., that need the help of a good trainer the most. Salsa was certainly difficult at first, but training a challenging animal and making a connection with her is very rewarding. When somebody tells me that an animal is "untrainable," I simply take that to mean that training may take more effort, extra time, or a special approach.

The Complex Contours of Advanced Training

What do we mean by "advanced training"? It's surprisingly hard to pin down. Are we talking about teaching a complex, multi-part skill? About working fluently under difficult circumstances? About teaching an animal to recognize abstract concepts like "largest" and "smallest"? About skills that demonstrate problem-solving at new levels? About the ability to train any species one encounters? The answer is all of the above.

The articles in this chapter focus on training goals, ideas, techniques, and concepts that stretched and changed my thinking. These experiences augment what most trainers know or can do. I investigate the idea of providing animals "choice," delve into the impact of collecting data on the effectiveness of training, discuss the controversy about using an "all clear" in scent-detection work, explore teaching dogs how to count, and demonstrate how pursuing complex training can transform animals. I often say, "Advanced training is just the basics done really, really, really well!" See if you agree. Whatever your opinion, I hope you see the limitless pathways that great training can open.

What Is Choice? The Evolution of a Concept

The concept of "giving animals choice" has become popular lately, but it is a relatively new and confusing concept for many. What do we mean when we say we are "giving animals choice"?

"Giving animals choice" is an ideal that trainers arrive at in stages; we are all at different points along the continuum of implementing the concept. In my experience, there are five common phases that trainers can go through when it comes to giving animals choice.

Phase 1: "Choice" is not useful in training and entails lack of control for the trainer.

Some trainers feel that animals work for them, and that it is the trainer's job to teach the animals to perform specific tasks: locate explosives, guide a blind person, find lost victims, and so on. These trainers worry that if they give animals choice, the animals may choose not to work—a realistic concern if training is not fun or is accomplished using punishment or coercion. This old-fashioned way of looking at the trainer-animal relationship still exists in some training circles today.

Phase 2: "Choice" is obtained automatically through positive reinforcement training.

Some trainers believe that choice is an inherent component of positive reinforcement training. While the use of positive reinforcement greatly increases the odds that the trainer is working in a paradigm of choice, it is not guaranteed. If an animal's lack of compliance means loss of reinforcement, the "choice" is sometimes a false or forced choice. For example, when we ask an animal to present a body part for a blood sample, he always has the choice to participate or not. When he cooperates, we might claim, "See, the animal doesn't mind this; he chose to cooperate." However, if the animal participated out of the fear that he might lose his dinner if he didn't participate, I would not consider that real choice.

Phase 3: "Choice" is ensured through "start-button" and "default" behaviors.

A new trend is teaching animals a start-button or default behavior that they can use to indicate to their trainers that they are ready to proceed with a behavior. Default behaviors create a better dialogue with an animal and give the animal control over outcomes, which is a powerful reinforcer. The use of these behaviors means nothing, however, if the behaviors are coerced. For example, consider using a chin-rest behavior for an animal to indicate that she is ready to proceed. If the trainer insists on the chin rest and refuses to provide any reinforcement until the animal gives the chin rest, then the chin rest is being coerced, and the purpose of the behavior is defeated. Instead, the trainer should retrain the chin-rest behavior and make it one that the animal wants to perform.

Phase 4: "Choice" is a product of an animal's reinforcement history.

In recent years, I have come to the realization that choice is a product of reinforcement history. When a behavior is reinforced often and well, the probability that the animal will perform that behavior willingly when asked is high. It could be argued that animals never have true choice, but the feeling and experience of choice can be engineered by a skilled trainer who takes the time to build an excellent reinforcement history.

Phase 5: "Choice" is strengthened by a good relationship and a dialogue with animals.

The best trainers achieve a good relationship with their animals through the use of reinforcement and the absence of coercion. Relationships improve when we are able to read and respond to an animal's body language and engage in a dialogue with the animal. It is only when we listen and adapt to animals that we can give them freedom to choose. A combination of a solid reinforcement history, a strong relationship, and clear communication gives learners the feeling of having choice.

Personally, I have never used the word "choice" to describe what I try to accomplish as a trainer. I think the word "choice" is the latest of many buzz words we use when we try to push for improved training and animal welfare. Ultimately, it is not the words we choose to describe what we do that matter most; the real test is an animal's welfare, health, and comfort. The best trainers continue to search for improvements and are seldom satisfied with the status quo. There will certainly be new phases and phrases in the years ahead as we keep striving to provide the very best care possible for animals.

Who Needs Data? We All Do!

Good trainers are doers! We enjoy interacting with animals and teaching new behaviors. However, most trainers are not great record-keepers. We often claim that we don't have time to keep records and don't really see the need.

I realize that I just made a sweeping generalization, which is certainly not representative of all trainers. But I come across the questions of the benefits of record-keeping and the importance of monitoring data frequently. During a recent trip to Europe, I found the need to address the benefits of good data with skeptical trainers on three separate occasions. I used the following examples to help illustrate my point and to convince trainers of the value of recording accurate data.

Narcotic-detection dogs

One group of trainers that does an admirable job at record-keeping and tracking data is drug enforcement K-9 officers. It's not that law enforcement trainers love record-keeping; they are not that different from other trainers. Rather, good record-keeping practices were developed out of a necessity; documentation is essential to combat attorneys representing individuals accused of drug possession. Defense lawyers in the United States are particularly adept at poking holes in drug-related arrests that result from the work of detection dogs, claiming that the search that led to the arrest was illegal. These lawyers hire former trainers as expert witnesses to discredit the way the narcotic-detection dogs were trained. They use the experts to find errors in the data to suggest that the dogs are not reliable. As law enforcement dog trainers began keeping better records, however, they were able to prove in court that their dogs were reliable.

In some of the early cases I was involved with, the defense lawyers had a point—not every dog was trained using the best practices to assure maximum success. Keeping better data allowed the trainers to analyze the strengths and weaknesses of their training protocols, which were then revised. As a result, the accuracy and reliability of their dogs greatly improved.

The clear improvement in detection accuracy also gave K9 officers more confidence going into court. These officers now had data that showed that their dogs had been trained, tested, and proofed against alerting on any substance other than the specific drug in question. Because of improved record-keeping, drug alerts made by well-trained narcotic dogs now hold up in court. Excellent training alone was not enough, of course. Trainers had to have the data to prove that the training was done correctly and that the dogs had been tested for accuracy in varied conditions with multiple distractions.

Zoo enrichment

In an effort to enhance the quality of life of the animals in their care, zoo staff members provide environmental enrichment for the animals. The enrichment may come in the form of food puzzles, toys, exercise games, and other creative options. The goals of enrichment vary from one group of animals to another and may include increasing use of certain parts of the habitat, increasing foraging activity, decreasing stereotypic behavior, and reducing aggressive behavior. If asked whether or not the enrichment they have provided has accomplished their goals, trainers usually reply with an emphatic "Yes!" But when asked how they know or whether they can prove it, the trainers find themselves at a loss about how to respond.

This problem is resolved, however, when the zoo staff members keep records and analyze the data. Thoughtful trainers conduct specially designed ethograms, which are scientific observations that help answer specific questions about an animal's, or group of animals', behavior. Before enrichment is offered, an ethogram is conducted to establish a behavioral baseline, such as use of space, aggressive incidents, minutes of stereotypic behavior, and so on. Then, after the staff provides enrichment, trainers repeat the ethograms and track changes in behavior. These data determine whether or not the enrichment has effected the desired change. The trainers can either prove that the enrichment is working or adjust their enrichment plan to achieve the desired result.

Aggression-reduction

I work with aggressive dogs regularly and have been involved in projects that assess whether former fighting dogs can be rehabilitated and adopted into families. There is no way to be certain that a dog with an aggressive history won't be triggered into an aggressive reaction, but when we implement a training plan designed to reduce aggression, there needs to be some concrete way to determine progress. We can feel as though we have made progress, but unless we track aggressive incidents and exposure to typical triggers very carefully, it is impossible to be sure.

With training as complex as aggression-reduction protocols, good data does so much more than just prove progress; it allows trainers to assess the efficacy of the training plan. Accurate data encourage the trainer to adjust the training plan and make sure that an appropriate plan is in place. Gathering this type of data is useful for more than just aggression management; it is useful for any type of problem-solving.

With difficult cases like fear, aggression, separation anxiety, and self-injurious behavior that take a long time to solve, both the trainer and the client can get discouraged and feel as if they are not making progress. But keeping track of incidents, frequency, intensity, recovery time, and other significant data will help everyone stay on course, see improvements, and not give up. It's easy to feel so busy, overworked, and underpaid that you do not see the immediate benefits of record-keeping. But creating graphs or before/after comparison charts will help your business and keep your clients happy.

General everyday use

If the only goal of your training is to teach your dog to sit or lie down when asked, detailed records are not important. But as you get more serious about results, record-keeping can help guide you to make more informed and accurate decisions.

Professional trainers use data records to improve training and help others see the value of tools and techniques. We often make sweeping claims about the benefits and drawbacks of certain training tools but, without data to back up those claims, we are simply stating opinions. One of the most compelling arguments to make to help people transition to the use of positive reinforcement is data; it is impressive to show data that illustrate the benefits of using positive reinforcement in various projects.

Until you see the benefits of record-keeping, it is easy to let it slide and avoid maintaining records. Once you are in the habit of good record-keeping and learn how to put the data to use, it does get easier. If it is used properly, documentation will help improve training by providing solid evidence of which techniques are most effective—and that information will ultimately help improve and advance our profession.

Ignorance Is Bliss: Real-world Use of Modifiers with a Search-and-Rescue Dog

Sometimes we venture into uncharted training territory without realizing how novel or new it might be. I had been teaching a graduate course on animal training at Western Illinois University since 1995. One of the students in my very first class was a firefighter named Bill who also trained search-and-rescue dogs. Throughout the semester, he asked great questions about the use of positive reinforcement because most of his experience was with the more traditional, correction-based training. After hearing about a technique that had been employed with dolphins or other zoo animals, Bill frequently asked, "Would that work with search-and-rescue dogs?"

My reply was always, "Of course it will; it works with all animals!" Although I had never worked with search-and-rescue dogs, I was confident in my answer because I had worked with many different species and always found the techniques successful. Although Bill came from the traditional world, he was not closed-minded, and he had great faith in me as an instructor and teacher. A few months after the semester ended, Bill called me and informed me that he was acquiring two new puppies destined to be search-and-rescue dogs. He asked if I would be willing to work with him to train these dogs using entirely positive reinforcement techniques! How could I refuse? I said yes and began a new friendship and an incredible new chapter in my life.

Bill and I spent the next two years together training his new German shepherd puppies as well as introducing the techniques to his experienced dog. In addition to typical searching and reporting tasks, we experimented with teaching the dogs modifier cues, cue combinations, and other conceptual skills. We taught them to discriminate between right and left, up and down, over and under, and large and small. The dogs learned to combine these modifier cues with other informational cues, such as find, retrieve, and touch, which became very useful in the field as we worked with the dogs in disaster settings. Only after we were well into the training did I find out that teaching conceptual skills was not conventional for search-and-rescue dogs. I had used these concepts with chimpanzees and dolphins, so we tried it with the dogs; I had no idea that no one had taught such cues in a search-and-rescue context previously, at least not to this extent. Because of the life-and-death reality of an actual search scenario—and the immense public scrutiny it would generate—we chose not to use these concept cues in the field until we were certain that the dogs would perform flawlessly in novel situations.

Bill continued to trust me as a trainer, and he had unwavering confidence in his dogs. Both were demonstrated one fall afternoon when we were at a disaster site where a building had collapsed. Before continuing with rescue efforts, the crew needed to acquire building blueprints. When we arrived on the site, a firefighter who had been in the building searching for the needed documents became trapped by falling debris. He was in the middle of describing where he was, and that it was unlikely the crew could get someone to him easily, when his radio went dead. We needed to find him and get a radio to him quickly. Bill suggested that his youngest female dog, Serena, would be up for the task. We strapped a radio to her collar and sent her in the proper direction, guiding her with verbal cues until she was out of sight, at which point her nose took over.

A few minutes later, the radio crackled and we heard the gravelly drawl of the trapped firefighter exclaim, "The pooch brought me the radio!" He went on to describe his situation and that, although he had found the location of the needed documents, they were on a shelf across the room that he could not reach because he was trapped. The documents were critical in determining the safest way to continue the rescue efforts.

While the captain and the firefighter discussed the dilemma, Bill pulled me aside brimming with excitement. "Ken, we can get Serena to get the documents!"

"How?" I asked.

Bill explained that we could get the firefighter to give Serena directions to retrieve the documents. I wasn't sure we were ready to put our new training to use; I was worried about wasting time and looking foolish. I tend to be a rather conservative trainer. We had not taught Serena to accept modifier and directional cues from strangers, and it seemed unlikely that Bill could give cues over the radio. Before I could argue my concerns further, Bill had already told the captain that Serena could get the documents. I cringed and shrank into the background as I watched Bill speak confidently to the firefighter over the radio and give cues to Serena through a man we had yet to even meet.

The documents we needed were in a binder on a bookshelf across the room from the trapped firefighter. Bill told the firefighter to relay, play by play over the radio, exact details of everything Serena did. Bill then gave the firefighter explicit instructions. We could not see what was taking place in that room buried beneath the rubble; we could only listen to the conversations over the radio.

Bill: Point to the wall and say, "Serena, Target!"

Firefighter (FF): Her nose is touching the wall!

Bill: Where are the documents in relation to where she is?

FF: On a shelf way over her head and to the right.

Bill: Tell her, "Right, Target!"

FF: She moved! But not enough.

Bill: Repeat it, "Right, Target!"

FF: She's pretty much right under the binder.

Bill: Good, now say clearly, "Target, Up!"

FF: Damn! That dog is smart! She's standin' against the bookshelf.

Bill: Is it the right shelf?

FF: No, it's on the next shelf up, but I think she could reach it.

Bill: OK. Call her name, say, "Serena, Come." She should come back to you. I want you to pet her and say, "Good girl. Good girl." Say it twice as you rub her. Then point to the wall again and say, "Serena, Target, Up."

FF: She went right back to where she was.

Bill: Good! Now tell her, "Up!"

FF: She moved to the next shelf! She f***in' moved to the next shelf!

Bill: How close is she to the binder?

FF: It's right in front of her.

Bill: Say, "Target!"

FF: She's touchin' the book right next to the binder. The binder is on her right.

Bill: Tell her, "Right, Target!"

FF: She's touchin' the damn binder.

Bill: Say, "Get it!"

FF: She pulled it halfway out and she sort of slipped down to the floor. Wait, she's back up on the shelf; she's pullin' it all the way out! (Crash) The book's on the floor.

Bill: Say, "Serena, Get it!

FF: I got it! The damn dog brought me the binder!

Bill: Say, "Good girl" and pet her.

FF: Damn straight I'm sayin' "Good girl!"

The firefighter got out safely, and we were able to complete a search of the entire building, saving 15 other trapped people.

I was amazed and pleased at Serena's ability to take cues from a stranger and to carry out tasks in such a novel environment. While we had put a lot of time into training, I marveled at Bill's confidence. We had accomplished a remarkable feat, but had we known that it had never been done, we might not have ever tried to train it. We probably would have thought the training would be a waste of time.

Our animals are capable of amazing things, more than we often give them credit for. In our case, ignorance was bliss and it led us down a rewarding path. Experiences like this continue to reinforce my interest in concept training and prompt me to keep exploring how much our dogs are capable of learning. I believe that if we continue to make training fun, the use of positive reinforcement will continue to open new doors for our learners.

Using an All Clear in Scent Detection—Lessons from Science

Scent-detection training has been receiving more attention in recent years. The use of dogs to alert on explosives has become increasingly critical in our ever-changing, politically charged world. New breakthroughs in medical-alert detection have created a demand for dogs that can assist patients with various medical conditions. Search-and-rescue dogs are still needed quite frequently; these dogs were perhaps some of the first dogs to use scent detection in critical ways. Although scent-detection training has been well-documented, many of the training techniques have not progressed much in the past few decades.

I have been helping with scent-detection projects for more than 15 years and often have been asked to solve recurring problems or challenges common in scent-detection programs. It is important to remember that dogs are already experts at the task of scent detection. Our role as trainers is to teach them which scent to find, when to find it, and what to do when they find it. In reality, the task of teaching a dog to alert on scent is pretty basic and straightforward; it is actually a minor part of the overall task. The most difficult aspects of scent-detection training fall into two categories: desensitization to working in the real world and our inability to actually smell the odor ourselves.

Our noses are not as good

In scent detection, we have to teach our dogs to be reliable enough that we can trust them when they tell us that the odor is present. Equally important is trusting that when the dogs do not alert that means no odor is present. This confidence becomes critical in real-world scent detection. When a dog misses a find (fails to alert when odor is actually present), there can be serious consequences:

- For search and rescue, a missed find can mean that a lost or trapped victim is not rescued and may die.
- In explosive detection, a missed find can result in a bomb being left armed.
- With a medical alert, a missed find can leave a sick patient unaware and unprepared for a medical incident.

Both false alerts (indicating that odor is present when it is not) and missed finds are problematic. All principled scent-detection trainers take these challenges seriously.

Problems with typical scent-detection protocols

Most scent-detection dogs are trained to alert only when they find an odor. If an explosive-detection dog is asked to search an area, the dog will sit and stare at the source of odor when explosives are detected; if no odor is detected, the dog keeps searching and is not expected to offer any specific behavior. In many cases, once the search of an area is completed and the dog finds nothing, he is asked to move to a new area and keep searching. In real-world searches, explosives are rarely present, so the dog is asked to search area after area with absolutely no reinforcement. There is no correct response other than to keep working. No wonder the dog gets frustrated! Some trainers do give dogs a rest or offer some other type of reinforcement between search areas, but rarely does a dog receive his favorite reinforcer (usually a ball or other toy)—except when explosives are actually found.

Teaching an all-clear alert

I have suggested that if teams trained an all-clear alert, the dog would always have a correct behavioral response: one alert indicating that odor is present and a different alert (an all-clear alert) to indicate that no odor is present. In this scenario, each time the dog is asked to search an area there is always a correct answer. While the addition of the all-clear behavior seemed clear and helpful to me, it was so different from the existing norm that the idea met significant resistance. In an effort to convince trainers and organizations of the efficacy of the all-clear signal, I suggested to several of the agencies I consult with that we conduct an in-depth review of the research literature and run some experimental training trials with a few selected dogs.

A look at the science

I have worked on a number of research projects in my career that utilized a variety of investigative paradigms to help answer questions about how an animal or person perceives their world. Three of the paradigms that I thought would be useful for increasing the understanding of scent-detection training are "match-to-sample," "two-choice," and "go, no-go." These paradigms are well-documented research procedures that ensure that the information we receive from studies is accurate and unbiased.

Matching to sample

Match-to-sample is a study technique that teaches the learner to perceive something (the sample), and then to find something else that matches the original sample. This procedure is used to test vision, smell, touch, hearing, taste, and almost any other sense that we want to investigate. It allows the investigator to determine the depth or complexity of an animal's sensory abilities reliably.

When we teach a dog to find a specific odor, we are using the equivalent of a match-to-sample paradigm. The dog is taught to recognize a specific odor (explosives, narcotics, a person, low blood sugar, and so on), and alert us when a matching scent is found. By looking at matching-to-sample studies, I felt my law-enforcement clients could find the most reliable way of teaching scent detection so that the accuracy of the alerts was as high as possible.

Go/No-go paradigm

Go/no-go is a procedure that tests subjects' perceptions by asking them to perform a specific behavior if they perceive whatever is being tested in the investigation. Conversely, if the subjects do not perceive anything, they are not expected to do anything in particular. This type of test is often used to evaluate a person's hearing. The individual being tested wears headphones and is asked to raise either the right or left hand depending on which ear hears a sound when it is played. If the person does not hear a sound, no action is expected. This is a typical Go (raise your hand if you hear a sound)/No-go (do nothing if you don't) type of study.

The biggest drawback to using this method in hearing evaluations is that when the sound begins to get outside of the individual's hearing range and s/he hears nothing for too long, many study participants begin to raise their hands randomly even though no sound is being played. Researchers have discovered that this is a typical test phenomenon. Presumably, the person does not want to get the "wrong" answer and begins guessing or thinking he or she hears something, even though no sound is being played. In animal studies, the researchers discovered that they had to work extra hard to make sure the animal was not "lying" in an effort to get more reinforcement. To me, this weakness of the go/no-go procedure resembled the challenges of typical scent-detection work, and could be a likely cause of false alerts.

Two-choice paradigm

In two-choice paradigms, the subject is asked to choose between two possible answers. This particular paradigm was invented to eliminate the uncertainty that the go/no-go paradigm often creates. In many research settings, the two choices are set up as "yes" or "no" answers. In redesigned hearing tests, the subjects are asked to touch a yes or no paddle to indicate if they hear a tone each time a light is illuminated in front of them. The light becomes the cue to touch a paddle and is, in effect, asking the question, "Do you hear a sound now?" The subjects wait for the light and then touch the appropriate paddle depending on whether or not they hear a tone. The subject always has an active option, a behavior to offer, no matter which answer is chosen. In these studies, the subject's answers were more consistently reliable and "honest."

The lack of accuracy in the results of go/no-go studies prompted me to suggest changing the approach to explosive-detection training. Give the dogs a "yes" (I smell odor) and a "no" (all-clear, no odor present) behavior so that they always have a correct answer available to them in every search area.

Improved reliability

In the testing that we have done with more than 30 dogs in several scent-detection contexts, teaching an odor-alert behavior combined with an all-clear behavior has been remarkably successful at reducing both false alerts and missed finds. (Anecdotally, it has also seemed to increase the dogs' enthusiasm for the searching and alerting tasks.)

The results have been quantifiable in real-world explosive-detection trials, with success rates averaging consistently above 95%. Previous data for real-world detection in some organizations were barely averaging 80%. Data have been presented at relevant law enforcement conferences, allowing various units to look at the information and decide for themselves about future use of this concept. But I am hopeful that those looking at scent detection in any context will consider the data that exist in the research community about the various research paradigms. This information is not new, and it gives clear evidence that there are techniques available to us as trainers that are well-documented and successful, and that might be useful in some of the new training applications that we develop for our animals.

Medical-alert detection

Working with medical-alert dogs is a slightly different situation. Unlike an explosive-detection dog that is cued to search an area and report, most medical-alert dogs are not cued *when* to alert. The medical-alert dog is expected to alert at any and all times, even when not cued to do so, specifically whenever the dog detects the odor she has been trained to find (for instance, low blood sugar for a diabetic-alert dog). This requirement would make the go/no-go paradigm seem like the preferred approach in training medical alerts. Various organizations report in their early work, however, that using a two-choice paradigm during the early stages of training sets the dog up for greater success.

Throughout her working career, the dog alerts whenever she detects the desired odor without being cued, in effect operating within a go/no-go paradigm. But, from time to time, the trainer can still ask if odor is present, which allows the dog to maintain the yes/no response as well—and keep her motivation and accuracy high.

Training medical-alert dogs is still new and developing work in many organizations. As we begin to share information about successful techniques, all of us who work with scent detection will become better informed. Ultimately, the animals will benefit from this shared learning and progress, as will any humans the dogs' scent-detection skills can help.

Keep studying, learning, and sharing

I will continue to write about the work I am doing in scent-detection circles and keep abreast of the work being done by others. My goal is to stimulate some thought about future exploration for people working in similar fields. I encourage all trainers who work on scent-detection projects to share their experiences, successes, and failures. I hope trainers will keep an open mind and look at options and alternatives that will continue to improve the techniques we use to train scent-detection behaviors. We should always set up our animals for success; make the goals clear and learning will be fun for the animals. Reliability will increase as well. Ultimately, in many of the contexts where scent-detection work is being used, the animals will be happier and lives will be saved—a win for all involved!

The Power of Ongoing Learning

In "The Unexpected Benefits of Training" (p. 205), I write about some well-trained, problem-solving animals and the incredible things they accomplished on their own. Here, I'd like to share a few amazing behavioral transformations I've seen in my work with rescued dogs. I believe that exposure to complex training tasks helps resolve many behavioral challenges that animals face. The exposure may prepare dogs to cope with the world a bit better. The more training animals receive, the more resilient they become, the more confidence they gain, and the more innovative behavior they demonstrate.

I have worked with many dogs that had severe aggression problems. Most were destined to be euthanized because shelter personnel deemed them too difficult to rehabilitate. I am often brought into these cases as an advisor.

Advanced training and long-term success

Given the proper tools, training, and environment, animals can learn solid skills that help their behavior evolve in a desirable direction naturally. I have observed that once a solid foundation for learning and behavior is put in place using positive reinforcement, and it is combined with complex learning taught by a skilled trainer, animals will develop desired behavior even when the main focus of later training is not directed toward the original problem behavior.

Here is the successful model I have seen repeated many times:

1. Animal is in a shelter due to various types of severe aggression.
2. Some type of context-specific, aggression-reduction training protocol is implemented successfully.
3. Animal is adopted into a stable, loving home where exposure to triggers is minimized.
4. Ongoing training and maintenance of behavior using positive reinforcement is practiced.
5. High-level, advanced training is implemented with dog for at least one year while avoiding exposure to aggression triggers.
6. After several years, aggressive behavior is gone or greatly reduced in untrained contexts.

Conversely, I have seen that when Step 5 is missing—there is no advanced, complex, or specialized training that stretches the animal's thinking—the animal's aggression in new contexts usually does not improve. I have witnessed this difference so many times that I believe there must be a correlation between the advanced training during a period of no exposure to triggers and the reduction in an animal's aggressive repertoire.

All of these cases began with well-designed, aggression-treatment protocols, giving the animals a solid foundation. Once in a stable home, the trainers were careful not to give the animals an opportunity to rehearse aggressive behavior. Other than wise management, they implemented no aggression-specific protocols. Yet, over time, the undesirable aggression faded away.

I present these case studies simply as food for thought.

Mickey

Mickey is a pit-bull terrier and former fighting dog that exhibited severe aggression easily triggered by other dogs and by most men. His aggression was managed through the application of counter-conditioning and desensitization techniques. He was adopted by a professional search-and-rescue dog trainer named Jim. Mickey's aggression treatment was focused on becoming comfortable in his new home and living with the dogs already in that household. Mickey settled into that environment well, and Jim was able to make sure that Mickey did not encounter strange dogs or men. Mickey's aggression was under control and well-managed.

Jim began training Mickey to perform basic search-and-rescue skills, not to introduce him to rescue work but to keep him active and allow him to participate in social activity with Jim's other dogs. Mickey was a fast learner. Later on, Jim offered to let me use Mickey as part of an imitation project that I had initiated. Mickey became quite proficient at copying the behavior of other dogs, and the project really stretched his cognitive abilities.

After 18 months in his new home, Mickey was out in the field with Jim's other dogs when they had an unexpected encounter with three unknown dogs and two men. Jim was surprised that Mickey exhibited no aggressive behavior; Mickey simply ran to Jim looking confused. Jim reinforced Mickey and moved him away from the strangers. A few months later, they had another surprise encounter with similar results, something that would not have been possible when Mickey first moved to his new home.

Because of those positive reactions, Jim began to introduce Mickey to new dogs and men, carefully and deliberately. I suggested that Jim keep track of the interactions and document Mickey's responses. Over the next several years, Mickey had more than 50 encounters with men or dogs that previously would have sparked severe reactivity. In all of those encounters, there were only four instances of mild barking, which subsided quickly and did not manifest in any aggressive behavior.

Mellie

Mellie, a bouncy Rottweiler mix that had been confiscated from a fighting-dog ring, was distrustful and aggressive toward all dogs. Leanne, a professional trainer who assisted the local shelter with severe aggression cases, treated Mellie for her reactivity issues using Emma Parsons' *Click to Calm* approach. Gradually, Mellie was exposed to new dogs below threshold and reinforced for accepting those dogs. This introduction procedure used a combination of counter-conditioning and redirection strategies.

Leanne fell in love with Mellie and decided to adopt her. Leanne was also an agility competitor, with three dogs at home. Although Mellie was still reactive to many dogs, she had progressed far enough that her training was focused on simply getting to know Leanne's other dogs. Leanne lived on a farm and could control Mellie's exposure to triggers easily.

Leanne introduced Mellie to agility training, which gave Mellie an outlet for her unbounded energy. Leanne also started using Mellie as a demo dog for her students. Mellie became one of the dogs the students could use to practice their skills. Mellie seemed to love the challenge of working with new people. Being a trainer-dog required patience and taught Mellie to generalize to constantly changing training styles.

Due to several personal changes in Leanne's life, she had to relocate to the city. Mellie had lived on the farm for three years and had not been exposed to strange dogs in all that time, but in her new living environment, she was suddenly and regularly exposed to new dogs. Much to Leanne's surprise, Mellie did not react with the severe barking that had been normal for her.

She seemed anxious and nervous, but Leanne was able to use redirection and high rates of reinforcement offered immediately to get through those situations. During their first nine months in the city, Mellie had hundreds of encounters that previously would have triggered aggression. In all of those encounters, Mellie had a mild growling reaction on just three occasions but was easily redirected.

Coral

Coral is a high-energy Airedale mix that had been given up to shelters by two different families due to severe reactivity to people, dogs, vehicles, wind-blown leaves, and almost anything that moved. She had bitten several people and was considered a high-risk dog. I decided to bring her into a formal training program, and she was treated for dog-reactivity through a cooperative training protocol that focused on desensitization to context-specific situations. Coral lived in a stable environment with three other dogs. She was cared for by a group of professional trainers, and she participated in educational programs and shows that were designed to teach people about pet adoption and the importance of training. Although reactivity was still an issue, it was managed by being careful not to expose Coral to things that were known to be triggers. She became stable as long as the environment remained stable.

In addition to daily show-training, I included Coral in a two-year quantity-recognition project that tested her cognitive skills significantly (see "1, 2, 3, 4... Can Dogs Count?" p. 103). During that project, she moved to a home environment where she was exposed to fewer triggers. Michele, one of her trainers on the project, adopted her, and Coral moved into a household with two other dogs. Michele continued Coral's training and began taking her to agility classes.

Coral had been through a lot in her life, but, as we assess her today, her reactivity issues have decreased in all but one context: exposure to rowdy kids. Coral is exposed to many of her other previous triggers, such as men, dogs, and bikes, several times daily, with no reactivity.

Bud

Bud is a nervous boxer that was highly reactive to loud noises and nervous in the presence of other dogs. He was treated for reactivity to other dogs with a cooperative training protocol, working with other dogs on opposite sides of a fence or gate. Bud became comfortable around other dogs but remained quite reactive to loud noises.

A social worker and child therapist named Theresa adopted Bud. Theresa lived alone but worked from her home, meeting troubled kids and their parents in her home for consults. Theresa spent a great deal of time training Bud on basic behaviors, and they did training sessions every day. They encountered other dogs on walks, and, although nervous, Bud was well-behaved. Theresa worked hard to prevent Bud from experiencing loud noises, but occasionally he would hear something and react adversely, growling, barking ferociously, and lunging toward the sound. While Theresa was seeing her clients, Bud was in other parts of the house, since many of her child clients could be rather unpredictable and noisy.

Nine months after adopting Bud, Theresa was hospitalized and was bedridden for nearly six months. A trainer friend of hers, Safia, came into Theresa's home to care for Theresa and Bud. Safia was a graduate student working on her master's thesis on dog behavior. She asked Theresa if she could use Bud for a series of matching-to-sample studies. These studies continued for more than a year, and Bud excelled.

Theresa was eventually able to start seeing clients in her home again. By chance, she happened to have a string of troubled children who exhibited quite violent behavior: yelling, screaming, having tantrums, stomping on the floor, or throwing things across the room. After one particularly intense and loud incident, with an object being thrown against the door to the back room where Bud was housed, Theresa realized that Bud was surprisingly quiet. A few months later, while they were walking down the street, a loud firecracker went off near them. Theresa and Bud both jumped back and were startled, but Bud did not bark or growl. Today, Theresa uses Bud to socialize with many of her pediatric clients. Some of these kids yell or make other sudden noises, at which point Bud just moves to the other room. He no longer demonstrates aggressive behavior around loud noises. Theresa estimates that Bud hears loud and surprising noises three or four times each month, but for the last two years, he has had no aggressive reactions to those sounds other than to look toward them and move away.

Further investigation needed

I have worked with dozens and dozens of aggressive dogs. The most impressive changes have occurred with dogs that have had a lengthy break from exposure to triggers combined with lots of fun, advanced training as part of a stable program. When that advanced training is not part of the equation, most of the dogs I've worked with continue to have aggression challenges.

In the cases I have presented, the aggression problems diminished because of a combination of factors: a good initial treatment protocol, a stable loving home, a long break from the triggers, a positive-reinforcement training environment, ongoing daily training, fun advanced training, and the passage of time. It is impossible to separate each of these components. As I compare the cases above with similar cases that did not include the advanced training element, I can't help but make the connection. The advanced training alone did not solve the aggression problem, but did it stretch the dogs' abilities and help them become more adaptable, confident, and accepting of changes? It is a question that I think requires further investigation.

We know training is beneficial. I present the cases of Mickey, Mellie, Coral, and Bud to open a dialogue and to encourage further investigation into this phenomenon. I look forward to hearing from others who have experienced similar transformations.

1, 2, 3, 4... Can Dogs Count?

I've always been fascinated by the cognitive abilities of animals. I used to teach a graduate course on animal intelligence. The popularity of the course was indicative of how interested people are in this topic.

Throughout my career I've been fortunate to work on a number of cognitive studies. I've co-designed studies on echolocation in dolphins, on match-to-sample[1] with a sea lion, and on imitation in dogs. In most cases, however, I was not the researcher but the trainer, helping cognitive scientists train various species to participate in projects. I learned first-hand that the scientific peer-review process is a rigorous, but necessary, step to validate that research is conducted properly.

Over the past 15 years my exposure to scientific research led to my interest in conceptual training with dogs. At the start, my focus wasn't on research but on having fun with the animals and helping others train concepts such as modifiers[2], adduction[3], matching-to-sample, and mimicry[4]. It was only after many years of teaching people how to train these concepts that I became acutely aware of the lack of published information on some aspects of the cognitive abilities of dogs.

In 2013, I began what I thought would be a brief project: train a few dogs to understand the concept of counting. Previously, I had trained several dogs to count to three, a task that is not particularly difficult. Science has shown that dogs have the ability to recognize quantities of three easily. I had no idea where this journey would take me over the next several years! It certainly would not have been possible without my enthusiastic partner, Coral, a three-year-old, highly reactive, rescued Airedale mix.

Phase 1: Three objects

Coral learned to look at objects placed in a tray and then touch a target, indicating how many objects were in the tray. A blue circle indicated one object, a green rectangle indicated two, and a black triangle indicated three. Essentially, the number of objects in the tray became Coral's cue, signaling which target shape she should touch. Coral achieved an accuracy rate of 98% over many trials.

At ClickerExpo 2014, I presented the early results of teaching Coral to count. It was a simple project, but many trainers were fascinated because they had not seen it trained previously. After my presentation, colleagues Dr. Susan Schneider and Dr. Susan Friedman, separately, gave me great feedback and suggestions for improving the project design and turning the project into publishable research. They both believed in the project and gently encouraged me to keep going, despite my insistence that I was not interested in taking the project further.

Phase 2: Eight objects in a double-blind setting

Six months later, I started over with the project, with a number of new protocols in place. This time, Coral learned to indicate the number of items in the tray by touching a whiteboard with magnetic dots on its surface. After Coral looked at the objects in the tray, she had to touch the whiteboard with the corresponding number of dots. To succeed at this, I presumed that Coral would have to "count" twice—first the items in the tray, and then the dots on the board.

I set up what scientists refer to as "double-blind trials" that prevented me from communicating the right answers to Coral unknowingly or biasing her responses in any way. These were the protocols used in a typical trial:

- I could not see the tray of objects or the person placing the objects, and never knew the correct answer to the question.
- Person #2 (who was placing objects in the tray) was not able to see the whiteboards and had no ability to prompt or assist Coral inadvertently as she picked the correct answer.
- Person #3, unseen by Coral, me, or Person #2, had a one-way view of the boards.
- The number of objects and the specific objects placed in the tray were determined randomly by a computer program.
- Each session consisted of 10 trials.
- The sequence of the boards was random and changed frequently in each session.
- The position of the dots on each board was changed regularly to guard against possible pattern recognition.

Each trial followed this sequence:

1. I gave Coral the cue "How Many?"
2. Coral poked her head into a curtained-off area, where a second person had placed a number of objects in the tray.
3. Coral then went to the white boards and made her selection by touching the target above the board of her choice.
4. The third person marked with a clicker if Coral made a correct choice.
5. I reinforced Coral if I heard the click. I did nothing if there was no click.
6. Either way, I set up Coral for another trial.

We progressed to the number 8. Coral's success remained above 95% for numbers 1 through 5 and dropped to 90% with numbers 6 through 8. These response rates were far above chance, and I felt certain that I was in a solid position to suggest that Coral had learned to count. I presented this work at ClickerExpo 2015 and received enthusiastic responses.

ClickerExpo faculty member Dr. Jesús Rosales-Ruiz invited me to present my canine counting research at an annual meeting of leading behavior analysts, educators, and students at the University of North Texas. While the audience members applauded the work I had done and acknowledged that Coral was doing something quite extraordinary, they doubted it could actually be called counting. Although I had a good double-blind set-up for trials, the audience helped me see where biases or other factors might be influencing Coral's responses and suggested that I research similar cognitive work that had been done with children. This idea helped me recognize that defining counting is neither easy nor clear. Cognitive psychologists still debate the term counting. No wonder I was having trouble convincing people that Coral was counting! The audience encouraged me to publish—with a few little tweaks.

Once again, I said that I had no interest in taking this project further. I had been thwarted and derailed several times in past years attempting to publish my work with imitation in dogs; it was not a process I was eager to go through again. There were other challenges to resolve. A loving home had adopted Coral. I had not seen her for a long time, and she was no longer part of a structured training program. Moreover, I did not have access to the training space where our previous training took place or to the staff who could assist me.

Despite these obstacles, a voice in my head said there would never be a better time. I had trained many dogs to count, but none had Coral's enthusiasm and focus. How could I not take advantage of her eagerness and discover how much more she could learn?

Phase 3: Match-to-sample counting

In the summer of 2015 I embarked on a new, and (I hoped) improved, phase of the counting project with the following significant changes:

- Using "matching-to-sample" as a mechanism to ask Coral multiple questions about a single set of objects placed in a tray
- Varying the size and shapes of the "dots" on the whiteboard to further interrupt possible pattern recognition
- Introducing Coral to multiple "new" or never-before-seen numbers in a single session with no pre-training

We tested Coral in trials that included as many as 22 objects. Preliminary data indicate that she achieved an accuracy rating of 79% with numbers up to 14. As we progressed to larger numbers, her accuracy began to drop quickly. Although she still performed with accuracy above chance, quantities higher than 14 began to frustrate Coral.

Interpreting the results

At ClickerExpo 2016, I presented my findings in a session called "Are You as Smart as a Dog?" I shared videos of the counting training, a representative sampling of the trials, and how what I had discovered about published studies of counting with children correlated with what I had learned about Coral's abilities. At this point it is difficult to draw any definite conclusions about counting in dogs, but Coral showed remarkable skill at quantities up to 14.

Is Coral actually counting? Is there any significance to the fact that she could recognize quantities of 14 easily but not higher than that? Does the fact that she was a highly reactive rescue dog affect these abilities? Did positive reinforcement training have an important influence on Coral's ability to learn as much as she did? Where should others take this information, and what additional research might this project prompt?

I believe that animals are capable of far more than we give them credit for. A good relationship with an enthusiastic animal, combined with a thoughtful training plan, can produce astonishing results. I am excited to share Coral's amazing journey and hope to work with others to take this project further.

Terms

[1]**Match-to-sample:** This is an established research technique that allows scientists to study a subject's sensory capabilities (vision, taste, smell, hearing, and more). In visual match-to-sample, for example, the subject is shown an object, a shape, a color, or some visual stimulus; the object is then removed and a set of two or more objects are presented. The subject must then indicate which of the objects, shapes, or colors is the same as the one shown earlier. Scent-detection dogs use olfactory match-to-sample to find or track people. I teach match-to-sample as a starting point for training more complex concepts.

[2]**Modifiers:** This is a concept that attempts to teach animals cues that are designed to modify normal behavioral activities. For example, if an animal is taught cues for "right" and "left" and then those cues are paired with already known behaviors, the animal should be able to take direction the first time those modifiers (right or left) are paired with a new behavior, without specifically training the animal to use right or left with that new behavior. Further clarification: if an animal spins right on the word "right" and spins left on the word "left," these words are not modifiers; they are just cues for one direction of a spin. However, if the animal understands conceptual modifiers, the trainer should be able to place two kennels side by side and cue "right kennel" or "left kennel" and the animal would enter the correct kennel. If the animal truly understands the concept of "right" and "left," the trainer should be able to pair the modifier with any behavior and give a new set of instructions. Other modifiers might include large and small, soft and hard, over and under, and so on. Numbers are actually an advanced type of modifier.

[3]**Adduction:** The combination of two or more behaviors to form a new behavior is called adduction. If you combine the behavior "down" with the behavior "come" you end up with a "crawl" behavior. If the animal learns to take the individual cues and combine them into the new behavior, that is considered a compound cue. It rises to the level of conceptual adduction when an animal can be given two cues for the very first time and perform the two behaviors simultaneously without previous training.

[4]**Mimicry:** When an animal can learn a behavior by imitating what another animal does, the process is called mimicry, or, more accurately, imitation. Teaching an animal to understand the concept of imitation is an advanced skill. True imitation can only be proven when an animal can do a behavior he has never in his life done before immediately after seeing another animal demonstrate the behavior. This is another area of research in which I have been active.

5 Species Unlimited

This book is full of stories about species beyond the domestic dog and about experiences that are definitely outside of normal training routines. This chapter's first two articles detail unexpected experiences with a bottlenose dolphin and a reindeer. The final three pieces are about conservation-related training—from a harrowing encounter with elephant poachers, to a beautiful experience training butterflies, to my suggestions to those who want to pursue the unique field of conservation training.

A Memorable Memory: The Story of Dolphin Zsa Zsa

In *Animal Training: Successful Animal Management through Positive Reinforcement*, I recount the story of Zsa Zsa, a bottlenose dolphin that was accidentally presented with a cue she had not seen in over a decade, yet she performed the behavior perfectly. That experience had several of us wondering just how good a dolphin's memory might be.

Zsa Zsa was more than 30 years old and had been in a community habitat in our facility since I had started working there 3 years earlier. Records indicated that she had not been in the show area and had not been asked for any of her old behaviors in at least 12 years. At that time all we did with her were basic feeding and stationing behaviors. One of our senior trainers had worked at our facility for 11 years and said that Zsa Zsa had been an older non-performing dolphin when he began more than a decade earlier.

One day we were surprised to find an old television program that featured our facility; the star of the dolphin show was named Zsa Zsa! None of us could believe that this was the same dolphin, but it certainly looked like her. Besides how many dolphins named Zsa Zsa could there be? The dolphin on the television show exhibited an amazing repertoire of behaviors—we all watched with our jaws agape!

We spent the next several weeks poring through old records. Unfortunately, record-keeping in those days was not as precise or thorough as it is today. We were able to confirm that Zsa Zsa—yes, *our* Zsa Zsa—had been a regular performer in shows 20 years previously. We could not find any list of her behavioral repertoire, any training records explaining how she was trained, or information about cues or criteria, but, with our curator's permission, we decided to see if we could determine how many of her old behaviors she might recall.

We watched the old television show at least 100 times. We listed every behavior that we saw in the show, a total of 22 behaviors we had never seen Zsa Zsa perform. We learned the cues from watching the trainer on the show and tried to determine criteria based on what we could see. Once we had completed our research, we decided that we would try a few cues at each session over the next few weeks and see how many behaviors Zsa Zsa might exhibit. We were hopeful that she might remember at least one or two!

We were excited and hopeful, but we never expected what was about to take place. I had the privilege of showing Zsa Zsa the first of the cues we had pieced together. I held my breath and gave her the cue for a porpoising behavior; she stared at me motionless for nearly five or six seconds. I was disappointed. It seemed as if the cue meant nothing to her. Suddenly, she took off with an energy we had seldom seen, swam underwater for a few seconds, then burst from the water into the air in a perfect porpoise—just as we had seen on the television show!

We squealed with excitement! I reinforced her well. Should we stop or keep going? Everyone encouraged me to try another behavior. I nervously gave her the cue for a forward tail walk. Again, she hesitated briefly and then glided across the water, holding the upper portion of her body in an upright position above the water, while her powerful tail propelled her forward!

Zsa Zsa zoomed back to me with enthusiasm and energy. I applauded and rubbed her on the melon and gave her a handful of fish. We had not planned to ask for more than two new behaviors in any one session, but everyone yelled, "Try another!"

So, I did! Fourteen additional times! Every behavior seemed perfect. Each time Zsa Zsa showed more and more enthusiasm. She was like a young dolphin; I'm not sure who was more excited, the staff or Zsa Zsa!

We stopped after 16 behaviors because I couldn't remember any more of her cues, but I bet Zsa Zsa would have! Over the next two days, she recalled 21 of the 22 behaviors! The behavior she didn't remember had a cue we could not see well on the television show; we were convinced it was our fault.

This little experiment had no scientific controls and may not prove anything specific about dolphin memory, but it is evidence of a good memory and of the joy and excitement that training creates for our animals. We thought retirement was the right thing for Zsa Zsa but realized she wanted the interaction that training provides. We added daily training sessions for the remainder of her life.

This interaction with Zsa Zsa took place nearly 40 years ago; times have changed and the idea of "retiring" animals when they get older is very different. Modern trainers adjust their training as animals get older, and we are careful to make sure we consider older animals' physical and mental needs. But we also recognize that animals trained with positive reinforcement usually enjoy interacting with their trainers. Many of the tasks they have been trained to do they consider fun and something they look forward to doing. This was a lesson I learned early in my career because of my interactions with the marvelous dolphin named Zsa Zsa.

Reindeer Games

While I was in Europe in 2016, I was invited to a zoological conference to present a talk on the importance of training for improved animal welfare. I had no plans for doing any training demonstrations during the conference, but I ended up conducting an impromptu training session with a male reindeer during a tour at a local zoo.

Several of us were admiring a herd of reindeer when a keeper entered the enclosure to do a late-afternoon cleaning. The keeper, Paolo, had to push away a large male reindeer that was getting too close for comfort. Paolo laughed as he explained that the male was very unruly and always got in the way during cleaning. One of the conference attendees said, "You should get Ken to train him."

Paolo replied, "Oh, he's not trainable."

"Ken says anything is trainable," shouted another attendee.

Paolo scoffed, "Love to see him try!"

I tried to focus on my zoo map and ignore the undesirable behavior of colleagues coaxing me into a training session. I don't normally like doing training demos with animals I don't know, especially when it comes in the form of a challenge. But it was too late; everyone was looking at me and asking me to try training this pushy reindeer. It was clear that I wasn't going to get out of doing something, so I decided to turn the situation into a problem-solving session. I asked Paolo why he thought this reindeer was not trainable. Paolo explained that the male reindeer always gets in the way during cleaning, which I was witnessing firsthand, and nothing could dissuade him from interfering and obstructing.

I pointed out that, because the male reindeer has so much interest in the keepers, we might be able to turn that into a good thing. I asked Paolo what he thought the reindeer wanted. Paolo explained that the male liked to lick the keeper's hands and arms. I commented, "It seems to me that this male either likes people or he's seeking the salty flavor of your skin—maybe both."

The zoo staff hadn't named their reindeer, so I decided to call this curious male Rudy. I asked Paolo, "What would you like Rudy to do when you're in the enclosure?" Paolo said that he just wanted to be left alone when he was working. I asked if I could use Rudy's remaining food as a reinforcer to try some training, but Paolo informed me that the reindeer had eaten for the day. The only possibility remaining was hay, which Rudy had been foraging on most of the afternoon.

While I was talking to Paolo I was standing outside the enclosure, leaning over the fence, and Rudy started trying to lick my hands. I said that I wasn't sure how well this would work, but since there was no food available, I was going to use Rudy's desire to lick me as a reinforcer.

I suggested that we pick a behavior for Rudy that would be acceptable to all of the keepers. After some discussion, we chose walking away from the keepers and standing by one of the large trees in the exhibit. The exhibit would serve as a station. I began by making a tongue click sound with my mouth and paired that sound with offering Rudy the opportunity to lick my hand. I did that five or six times, and then I started moving along the fence to see if Rudy would follow me. Rudy was focused on me and went where I went. I clicked my tongue, and then let him lick my hand. In just a few minutes, it was clear to me that he understood the meaning of the click.

Next, I decided to stop offering my hand to see how Rudy would respond. He stared at me for about 30 seconds, and then he pushed on the fence where I was standing. He looked a bit frustrated, and finally he turned to walk away. I let him get one step away from me, then I clicked my tongue and offered him my hand again, which he came back to lick eagerly. I pulled my hand away and waited; Rudy stared again, and finally he walked away. I let him walk a few steps further, then clicked and offered my hand. At that point, everyone watching laughed and clapped because they understood what I was doing. Most important, they could see Rudy responding to the training game and learning! (I was so tickled that this was working as well as it was. Talk about training under pressure!)

Over the next five minutes I trained Rudy to walk to a tree halfway across the habitat. Rudy was now running to the tree the minute I pulled my hand away, which had now become the cue to go to the tree. He would wait by the tree until I clicked, then come trotting back. Curiously, he always circled around the tree when he got there, which I thought was cute and accepted as part of the behavior. The entire training process occurred in less than 10 minutes.

The session became a very powerful demonstration of basic training and shaping; it illustrated the power of training as a communication tool between teacher and learner. I used the opportunity to talk to the group about redirection and finding incompatible behavior to replace unwanted behavior. The training also provided an excellent example of alternative reinforcers and how to use what the animal already finds reinforcing. I can't remember the last time I was put on the spot like that, but it reinforced the training message from my keynote talk the day before.

I ended up coming back to visit the reindeer habitat frequently that night. When Rudy saw me approaching, he ran straight to me. Rudy's enthusiasm was so funny to watch. Throughout the evening, conference attendees asked me to go visit the reindeer because they wanted to watch Rudy gallop over to greet me. It was a cool experience and a great reminder that training doesn't have to be complicated. The tools I used were very basic: good timing and appropriate reinforcers combined with observing and responding to the behavior and desires the animal demonstrates. And, the task was completed in a relatively short session. I hope that the zookeepers maintain the training that we started that night and that Rudy continues to join in his new reindeer games!

The Steep Price of Conservation

My pieces are usually training-related, but this time I want to share with you a personal story that affected me in a profound way. The details of the location and the names will be reserved for a full report later, when the project is complete and I can be sure that everyone is safe.

I've been involved in a number of conservation-training projects in my career. One of my recent projects has been to change the migration route of a large herd of elephants. The current route takes them through poacher territory and has resulted in the slaughter of dozens of elephants every year. The plan is to use remote training* (see below) to re-route the elephants and direct them to a safer path. The project requires multiple environmental-impact surveys, specialized permits, and a team of more than 150 people representing a dozen organizations. Several large conservation organizations are funding and monitoring the project. The project had been in the planning stages for more than four years, and was to begin in November of 2017, the start of the dry season and the time of the next elephant migration.

In June of 2017, I traveled to Africa and met with local park rangers who were key to organizing logistics onsite. The trip was a scouting mission to finalize important details, look at locations, and observe the elephants. I was greeted at the airport by a park ranger, whom I will refer to as Keller. Keller was my liaison with the ranger team, and he was going to be the onsite ground team leader in November. Keller proved to be a kind man, admired by his ranger team, a good leader, and very knowledgeable about the local elephant herds.

The next three days were magical. Keller and three members of his team escorted me to several sites where I observed the large herd. I watched mothers caring for their youngsters and observed these magnificent animals as they ate, bathed, and interacted with each other. Those were emotional and beautiful days.

As I watched the elephants, I was even more motivated, if that's possible, to make this project happen. If successful, the project had the potential to save 40 or 50 elephants every year for the foreseeable future. I felt angry that poachers were slaughtering these endangered animals in alarming numbers and proud that I might be able to play a small part in changing their fate. Keller and his ranger team members were equally motivated and thrilled that this project was getting underway.

On day four, we began a planned week-long trek along the annual elephant migration path. The goal was to introduce me to the terrain, look at planned locations for route changes, and discuss the behavior-adjustment plan in detail. I was amazed at the incredible landscape and the many animals along the route. I kept pinching myself to make certain that this was real and that the project was actually about to happen.

It was mid-morning, the heat of the day had not yet hit us, and our two jeeps were travelling along a bumpy dirt road when I heard a tat-tat-tat sound in the distance. I remember thinking, "I wonder if that's an African woodpecker." Then Keller, seated next to me in the driver's seat, yelled into his radio something about machine-gun fire. What happened next is a bit of a blur. Keller and the driver of the other jeep made sudden U-turns and we travelled at top speed toward a grove of trees. The tat-tat-tat sound continued and was followed by a loud explosion, which we later learned was the result of a rocket launcher. Our jeeps had no top and we were not wearing seat belts. I remember flying through the air and seeing the landscape spin around me, until I hit a tree and blacked out.

Much of what I share next was pieced together from conversations with my colleagues and the brief recollections of what happened over the next few hours and days. I awoke, perhaps a few minutes later, to see both jeeps overturned. One of them had sustained serious damage and had plumes of smoke drifting from the engine. The tat-tat-tat sound had stopped, and it was eerily quiet. I remember my whole body hurting, but I was able to stumble over to one of the jeeps and found one of the rangers trapped underneath it. Although I don't remember doing so, the ranger tells me that I lifted the jeep and pulled him to safety. This man weighs nearly 300 pounds, so I still find that story astonishing. If the story is true, I must have had a great deal of adrenaline rushing through me.

We managed to get all five of us together and we hid behind one of the jeeps, uncertain whether the attackers might still be nearby. We radioed for medical help, as it was clear that we had serious injuries to deal with. Keller and one other ranger had gunshot wounds, Keller's quite severe. We later discovered that the other two rangers had broken bones, and I had sustained a serious concussion, which complicated an existing medical condition and put me in some danger.

A medical helicopter finally arrived, along with two medics. There was only room in the helicopter to airlift two people at a time, so one of the medics stayed with us while the two rangers with gunshot wounds were taken to the hospital. We were a long way from a major city and a modern hospital, so it would be several hours before the helicopter could return and take the other two rangers and then, finally, come back for me. Since they were triaging, taking the most serious injuries first, I would not get to the hospital for many hours. The medics arranged for a vehicle to come in from a local village and drive me to a tribal doctor for care in the interim.

I remember that the tribal doctor had me write my emergency contact information on a piece of bark, which he put on a string and hung around my neck. Next, he said that he needed to "take off my hair." I remember being confused by that, but I slowly realized that he wanted to shave my head, which he did. He then took some large green leaves, dipped them in what seemed to be a plant-based medicated fluid, and strapped them to my now bald skull. This was a tribal remedy that I have yet to fully understand, perhaps meant to reduce inflammation. Approximately ten hours after the incident, I was airlifted to a hospital. Due to my complications, I was placed in a medical coma for several days. Thankfully, my treatment went well, and I made a speedy recovery.

Keller ended up being hospitalized for more than a month, as his gunshot wounds were serious and nearly cost him his life. I am happy to report that he is home and recovering well, although he is still not back at work. We have all kept in touch and are all, thankfully, on the road to a full recovery.

Investigation into the incident has indicated that the attack was probably planned by poachers who were trying to send us a message. As a team, we are examining safety precautions before we move forward with the next phase of the elephant-migration project.

Since the incident, one of our major funders has pulled out of the project. However, the other principal funders have stepped in to fill the void. The five of us involved in the attack agree that the project should move forward once safety and security issues have been resolved. When and how the project will proceed will not be made public, for obvious reasons.

The seriousness of this incident demonstrates just how determined poachers are and how lucrative poaching can be. Humans have a dramatic impact on this planet, and it is our responsibility to find ways to protect it. It is gratifying to me that my knowledge and skills as a trainer can be used for projects of this type. For now, I am just thankful to be able to write this update at all.

I have always had a great appreciation for how short life can be and for the need to live every day as if it is the last. This experience was a reminder not to put off for tomorrow what you can do today. When I wake up each day on The Ranch and take care of chores in the barn, clean up after the donkeys, train the alpacas, or give an affectionate scratch to the goats, I know I am lucky. I feel privileged to be able to do those things. I never want to lose track of what is important. Whether the project is large or small, I will continue to be grateful for the opportunities I have and to appreciate time for the gift that it is.

Project Update

I returned to Africa less than six months after the incident. I was embedded in a tourist group so that I could observe the migration and get back on the proverbial "horse." Security during migration season is exceptionally tight, so I felt safe. As an added precaution, I went in disguise, just in case poachers were looking for me. Going back was important for both practical and emotional reasons. It proved beneficial in that I was able to watch the full migration. It also allowed me to see how I would feel back in that environment, without the pressure of working and making important training decisions. Emotionally it was a hard two weeks, but I got through it and felt better prepared to begin the project in 2018.

The incident delayed the start of the project by one full year, but, ultimately, we were much better prepared. We were more aware of the risks and we had greater community buy-in. Volunteers from five tribal communities joined the project and were helpful in various aspects of the training and security plan. During the 2018 migration, we rerouted 374 elephants away from poacher territory successfully. From 2013 through 2017, an average of 64 elephants were lost from this particular herd (this average is a combination of poaching and natural deaths). After just one year of the project, the 2018 census indicated a loss of only 4 elephants (none from poaching). The permitting authorities were so pleased with our results that they extended our permit to continue the project through 2027. Our team is ecstatic about the results and we have made improvements and adjustments to our future plan. I look forward to publishing a full description of the project and the results once we have completed our work.

Note:

*Remote training is training in which the trainer does not interact with the learner directly. Reinforcers are delivered in creative ways that appear to come from the natural environment. For instance, PVC pipes can be hidden in a tree to deliver reinforcers when trainers push a button, or a remote feeding device can be set up to spit out kibble when triggered by the trainer watching on a webcam. This type of training is increasingly being employed in wildlife-conservation projects to prevent habituation or any contact whatsoever with humans. This technique also has increasing applications in pet management, since it can be used to help deal with separation anxiety and other behavioral challenges while a pet is alone at home.

The Butterfly Project

Over the years, I have had the good fortune to work with some amazing animals and incredibly talented people, and in a variety of unique and inspiring situations. So, when I say I have had an experience that was wonderfully special, that is saying a lot.

Can you show us how to train butterflies?

I was asked to participate in a special project that I will refer to as the London Butterfly Project. A botanical specialty group in the United Kingdom built a large garden designed to show the symbiotic relationship between plants and animals. Each year, this group sets up different gardens with different themes in different parts of the UK. Their focus for 2015 was to demonstrate the role that butterflies have in certain ecosystems. This project included more than 10,000 butterflies of many species that lived in the garden, which was hidden among the tall buildings of London. The garden occupied a space that was larger than a football field.

The director of the project, Lucinda Bartholomew, had envisioned a fund-raising gala presentation that would include an orchestra in the middle of the garden playing beautiful classical music while butterflies flew from one part of the garden to the other. She had heard of me through a mutual friend and contacted me to ask whether I thought thousands of butterflies could be trained to fly on cue, and in unison, from one location to another. I explained that I had never worked with butterflies and knew little about their sensory mechanisms, but I imagined that if someone understood those things, it should certainly be possible. Lucinda then followed up with the question: "Would you be interested in helping design and implement a training plan for our butterflies?" I immediately said yes! Train thousands of butterflies to fly from point A to point B on cue? What a unique training opportunity!

Now, how do I do it?

I began reading up on butterflies and sent a dozen questions to the group's butterfly specialists. Which of the butterfly senses are better: vision, hearing, smell, or something else? What do you feed them? How do you feed them? How often do they eat? Can you send me pictures of the garden? Can you show me where you want them to start and where you want them to fly to? The answers were varied, depending on the butterfly species. I found that some of the questions about the capabilities of butterflies were still being studied by scientists and are not fully understood for every species.

I also learned that some of the butterfly species are quite territorial and will compete and fight with other species for access to "their space." This characteristic worked to our advantage, since the butterflies had already self-selected their preferred spaces and were living in three different parts of the garden. Based on that information and combined with some other research, I proposed that we try to use three different cues: a vibrating subsonic cathode for one group of butterflies, a high-pitched whistling tone for another group, and a flashing light for the last group. Once I understood the goal of Lucinda's vision, I felt that we could make a bigger impression if we could train different groups to fly at different times. Project leaders loved the idea, and we moved forward with that plan—hoping that at least one of the cues would work with one of the groups.

Day 1: Training begins!

We began by using large bowls of fruit, nectar, and a special liquid solution ("butterfly food") depending on the species, and paired the selected cue (vibrating cathode, high-pitched tone, or flashing light) with the immediate presentation of multiple bowls of the preferred food.

We started with 25 of us (staff, volunteers, and me) spread out among the butterflies, with covered bowls placed next to the sources of the cue. The moment the cue was turned on, we removed the covers to the bowls, which were spread out over the areas where the butterflies were currently perched. (Do butterflies perch? Not so sure!)

We then moved to the next group of butterflies, pairing their unique cue with that group's food. We repeated the process with the third group. After about 25 minutes of feeding, we turned off the repeating cues, removed the bowls, and left for two hours. We followed this routine four times that day. At the third session, when the tone played, thousands of butterflies suddenly lifted in unison above their resting spot. It was so cool and kind of eerie, it gave me goosebumps! This was going to work! By the end of the first day the butterflies were flying to their food immediately upon presentation of the cue.

Day 2: Small approximations: move the bowls

On Day Two, we moved the bowls several meters away from where they had been placed on Day One. A majority of the butterflies made the short flight immediately! The team was amazed! For a while, I pretended that I was not surprised. After all, I always teach that training is the same, and works equally well, for all species, "whether training an earthworm or a Harvard graduate!" But I finally had to admit that even I was surprised at how well and how quickly this training worked. We were training butterflies successfully! *10,000 of them, at once!* (Well, maybe about 9,500 butterflies—there were still a few holdouts!)

Week 2: Butterfly bullies?

By the end of the second week, we had trained the majority of the butterflies to fly nearly 75 meters. We could have moved the first few groups the full 100 meters in this time frame, but we made smaller progressions because there were a handful of animals that did not learn as quickly. We took time to make the connection to the cue stronger for the stragglers, usually the less assertive of the butterflies. We accomplished this by spreading the landing sites over a slightly larger area so that the less assertive butterflies did not have to compete for food bowl space with the "bullies." (Who knew there were butterfly bullies?) After two weeks, we had reached a success rate with approximately 95% of the butterflies!

Week 5: Putting it all to music

On my last day in London, the team surprised me. They had me sit in the middle of the garden and just watch. A speaker system played a beautifully orchestrated classical symphony piece. About 45 seconds into the piece, the music began to swell, and right on cue all of the red and orange butterflies took off from the bushes and trees to my left. I watched in awe as approximately 2,000 red and orange colors fluttered across the space in front of me. The butterflies did not move fast but they moved in unison, and the group was spread out over several meters. They undulated in a beautiful tight formation and landed on the far right side of the garden.

Then there was another swell of music and about 2,500 purple and blue butterflies fluttered in a similar manner from the far left to another location on the far right. Then, just as the second group settled into their place, close to 5,000 butterflies of multiple colors took off from a location across from me and fluttered straight toward me and over my head, settling into their trees and bushes far behind me. There were tears in my eyes, and I was speechless! I had been so much in the middle of the process I had yet to truly appreciate how beautiful this behavior was. With the addition of the music, the butterflies appeared to undulate to the rhythm of the music—it was incredible!

Week 6-8: Maintaining the Behavior

The team had to maintain the behavior for another six weeks until the gala. There were still several approximations to make; the most difficult was getting these diurnal animals to make the flight at night. This was accomplished using special UV lighting throughout the stadium and moving the time of day later and later in 10-minute increments each day. The other surprise for me was finding out that some species of butterflies only live six weeks! I was crushed when I first learned this information a few days into the training with more than eight weeks to go until the gala. Fortunately, most of the species we were training lived longer than six weeks and there were new butterflies added to the population every day. The young butterflies that were added did not need to be trained, they simply followed the older butterflies each time the others took off. I had seen social facilitation at work but never relied on it so heavily in my training until now.

Week 9: The gala performance

Sadly, I was unable to fly back to London for the actual gala, but I still got to participate! I was in Chicago on the evening of the gala (actually, afternoon in Chicago, evening in London), and I dressed in a rented tuxedo and made my way to a television studio in downtown. Arrangements had been made for me to do a short speech about the butterfly training live via satellite to the group of dignitaries in attendance at the gala. After my speech, the cameras were rolling in London, and Lucinda had arranged for the entire proceedings to be sent live to my location. I remember sitting in that studio alone, with one technician making sure everything was working on my end. I sat on a stool in the middle of the studio, in my rented tux, staring at the big TV monitor. The orchestra began the first notes of the symphonic musical piece, I remember holding my breath for the full 45 seconds before the first flight. When the swell in the music played, the camera was focused on the string section of the orchestra. I panicked, and exhaled forcefully, "What, they're not going to show the butterflies?" But just as I spat out those words, the view on screen changed and there was this beautiful ribbon of orange and red undulating through the brightly lit night sky. The camera stayed focused on the ribbon for several seconds before cutting to a close-up of the butterflies—it was so beautiful. I watched all three flights be successful. I saw awe on the faces of the audience as the butterflies floated over their heads. I was filled with pride and I remember thinking, "I can't believe I trained this!" When it was all over, I sat on that stool speechless, eyes filled with tears. The studio technician asked, "Hey, buddy, you okay?" But I was too choked up to answer, so I just nodded my head and left the studio in a trance.

A project I will never forget

The project was an incredible success. I made new friends and had an unforgettable experience. The training process and the final gala performance were filmed by a British film crew for a documentary! The documentary has been several years in the making, but I have seen the rough cut, and it is a thing of beauty. For the gala, the botanic garden gave attendees a souvenir program; there was an entire page dedicated to me with my picture and my bio. But the thing that struck me was the title they gave me in the program: "Butterfly Trainer and Butterfly Flight Designer." Even for me, that was a unique entry for my resume.

Conservation Training

One of my greatest passions is conservation training; I lecture about this topic at every opportunity. I always end my talks with a call to action, inviting more experienced trainers to get involved in this type of conservation work. I am gratified when people approach me afterward to ask how they can get started. After a few years of answering each question as it came, it finally occurred to me to share my answers with a wider audience through my monthly Letter.

What is conservation training?

Conservation training is the use of behavior science to benefit wildlife conservation, either directly or indirectly. Here are a few examples:

Training animals to allow the collection of biological samples that can be used in conservation projects

My first exposure to conservation training occurred when I worked with marine mammals at Marineworld of Texas. Our team was approached by scientists who were seeking to understand an unexplained die-off of wild bottle-nosed dolphins in the Gulf of Mexico. The scientists needed blood samples from a healthy population to use as a baseline for comparison with the sick and dying animals in the wild. My team and I trained our dolphins to offer us their tails for the required blood samples. Our work led to eventual policy and management changes. It was a thrill knowing that I had contributed to scientific work that improved the well-being of wild dolphin populations!

Testing devices and protocols in a controlled setting prior to them being used by biologists with animals in the wild

While I worked at the Shedd Aquarium, I collaborated with researchers who wanted to design a tracking device for beluga whales for monitoring their movement and migration patterns in the wild. Over several years, I trained two belugas at the facility to wear the devices on their pectoral fins while the designers adjusted the comfort and functionality of the trackers until the trackers were put to use on wild belugas.

Remote training

One of my favorite types of conservation training is training in which the trainer is not perceived by the animals to be part of the learning process. My first exposure to this type of training was during the Exxon Valdez oil spill in 1989, when I participated in the rescue, rehabilitation, and release of oiled sea otters. After the otters were rescued, cleaned, and nursed back to health, they could not immediately be released because oil still contaminated their natural habitat. We needed to care for these animals for several months without habituating them to people. We wanted the animals to maintain their fear of people so that they would not become a nuisance to fishermen and boaters after their release (other releases in the past and since then have resulted in sea otters begging for food at fishing boats, climbing onto boats, jumping on kayaks, and biting people on multiple occasions, putting both people and sea otters at risk). Food, toys, and other reinforcers could not be perceived as coming from us.

We used underwater tubes to deliver the reinforcers to the otters while training them to go through a gate or step on a scale for weights. The otters only saw people when they were being restrained or handled for a medical procedure. More than 300 sea otters were released after the oil spill cleanup, and their successful integration back into the wild was a testament to the good use of remote training procedures.

In the last few decades, I have used remote training techniques in a variety of unique projects: my team and I taught chimpanzees in Sierra Leone to scream in unison as an alarm call when poachers threatened them in their habitat; I used remote training to help guide polar bears in Alaska away from villages and toward better food sources; and, currently, I am working with a team in Zambia on changing an elephant herd's migration route to avoid poachers. These are just a few examples of the remarkable ways in which remote training can assist animals in the wild.

Using dogs and their scent-detecting abilities to aid in conservation projects

Scent-detection dogs are often used for search-and-rescue work, explosive detection, and narcotic detection; conservation is a new and exciting application of this type of training. Scent-detection dogs are used for an array of conservation projects: detecting invasive zebra mussels, which can wreak havoc on local ecosystems, on ships before they are cleared to enter port; helping find the dens of endangered lizard species so that researchers can count and monitor the waning population; detecting sea-turtle nests at oil-polluted beaches so that the eggs can be dug up and relocated to safe hatching sites; finding rare or ecologically important animal scat; and more. I am excited to see the new and creative applications where scent-detection dogs will be used in the future!

Where to start?

There is no easy or clear path to lead trainers into conservation training. Each trainer must create his or her own path and explore options that are specific to personal interests and talents. I am a big believer in research, preparation, hard work, and initiative. What follows are some suggestions to get you started.

Expand your training skill

Conservation training requires creativity and an ability to work in unique and less-than-ideal situations. First, gain as much training experience as you can. I encourage all trainers, no matter your long-term goals, to keep stretching your training skills! Be creative, even if you only have one pet at home and no access to other animals. Here are a few ideas to get your imagination flowing:

- *Train a new behavior with your pet every day.* Keep your training sessions fun so that your dog, cat, or horse looks forward to each new session.
- *Try new things when you feel you and your animal are ready.* Try longer durations, work from a distance, present cues in a new manner, work in new environments. Keep challenging yourself to train more difficult tasks.
- *Offer your training services to friends, family, and neighbors.* Work with new animals whenever you can and find different species and different types of environments to enhance your experience.
- *Give yourself remote training challenges.* Set up a webcam that allows you to watch your animal, and then try to train some behaviors while in another room or in another location completely. How will you reinforce the animal? How can you set up the environment for success? Give yourself easy challenges at first and make them more difficult as you gain experience.
- *Train basic scent-detection tasks.* Teach your dog to play scent-detection games and increase the difficulty of the task as you and your dog gain experience.

- *Volunteer for a shelter or a small zoo that will allow you to try some basic training with their animals.* Not every organization will be open to this idea, but it never hurts to ask. Even if you only assist and watch trainers work with other animals, it will expose you to new ideas and techniques.
- *Teach your friends and family to work with your pet.* Improve your communication skills, discover what happens when someone else works your animal, and become comfortable transferring skills and techniques to non-trainers.

There really is no limit to the many ways you can keep pushing your skills. This list is just a place for you to start.

Expand your knowledge

Continue to expand your understanding of behavior science and the ways in which trainers apply it. Learn more about conservation projects and organizations. There are many ways to stretch your knowledge:

- Take classes, attend seminars, go to conferences
- Follow behaviorists, training organizations, leading trainers, and conservation groups on social media
- Join professional organizations, follow the organizations' publications, and keep track of trends in the field
- Read behavior literature, both scientific and practical
- Read about conservation issues and familiarize yourself with the types of conservation projects that are already underway
- Keep track of the organizations that are involved in conservation work: universities, not-for-profit foundations, zoological organizations, etc.

Do your research

When I started, I followed the work of various zoos active in conservation work. I became a member of international wildlife conservation groups and devoured every article about conservation initiatives and challenges they faced. I volunteered at a zoo so I could learn about the animals up close. It is up to you to keep track of conservation concerns and efforts with species that interest you. Join wildlife conservation organizations that appeal to you and follow their activities. Keep up to date with the challenges that species of interest to you are facing in the wild. Look for opportunities to participate in conservation work, either as an environmental tourist or as a volunteer for local data collectors.

Listed below are a few organizations where you can start your search for information, but these are only a few of many. Narrow your search by focusing on specific organizations that do the type of work that interests you most. When there are major conservation issues facing certain communities, there will often be public community meetings held to share plans and needs with that community; sitting in on these meetings can introduce you to the important players in that region and expose you to the politics and challenges of conservation work.

Create your own path

Ultimately, it is up to you to find opportunities—they will rarely come to you. When you approach organizations in your search for opportunities, you will often be directed to a membership or fundraising division, because that is where they can use the most help and that is where the majority of people provide the best assistance. Investigate further and determine if there are opportunities for you to use your unique skills. Most organizations will not see a need for animal-training assistance. In the majority of cases where I was able to help, training ended up being a last resort and it was only considered when all other options had failed. It may be easiest to get your foot in the door by offering to assist in other ways. Most organizations use volunteers for menial labor, food preparation, data collection, or other odd jobs. Don't be picky—any way you can assist serves a function and gets you involved in the organization. You may get rejected or turned away often, but don't let that discourage you. Look for another avenue or a different organization. Your interactions with these organizations should always be polite and respectful. Don't become a pest or the door to working with that organization may be closed permanently. If you start communicating with an organization that seems like a promising opportunity for you in the future, stay in contact. Be politely persistent (but not too persistent!)

Successful conservation work is time-consuming and requires a huge team effort; becoming part of a conservation organization's work takes the same effort. Lack of success at the start should not discourage you. It takes persistence. Remember that good conservation work is far bigger and more involved than being on the front line, working in the field; help is needed making phone calls, filing papers, logging data, and with dozens of other unglamorous tasks. If you are not willing to take on some of those tasks, it is probably best not to pursue conservation work, because that is the path that you may need to take to do the work that ultimately interests you. My first conservation project out in the field was the sea otter project I described above. It took 12 years of volunteering and working at other jobs before I acquired the skills and experience necessary to land me there. So, if you are looking for a short cut, I am not aware of one. If conservation work is important to you, be ready to take on lots of ancillary tasks to start. If, however, you follow the advice above and look into some of the resources below, you can make a difference!

Resources

This list is neither comprehensive nor all inclusive. I am providing these resources as a starting point, a way to generate ideas and get you thinking along the right lines. There are many more resources out there, so take some time to investigate on your own! For ease of use, you can link to this piece as it appeared on the clickertraining.com website (https://clickertraining.com/conservation-training) and gain direct access to all these links.

Conservation News Websites

Mongabay: News and Inspiration from Nature's Frontline:

https://news.mongabay.com/

The link below is an article on Mongabay about changing an elephant herd's migration route to avoid poachers:

https://news.mongabay.com/2018/04/animal-trainers-are-teaching-wildlife-to-conserve-themselves/

Most major news outlets have conservation focused divisions that you can follow: BBC, CNN, etc.

Conservation Dog Organizations

Working Dogs for Conservation, Boseman Montana: https://wd4c.org/

Conservation Canines, Center for Conservation Biology, University of Washington, Seattle, WA: http://conservationbiology.uw.edu/conservation-canines/

Conservation Dogs, in the UK: http://conservationdogs.com/

Canine Detection Unit, African Wildlife Foundation, Washington, D.C. and throughout Africa: https://www.awf.org/projects/canine-detection-unit

Articles about Conservation Dog Work

Do you have what it takes to be a conservation dog handler? http://www.animaljobsdigest.com/a-career-as-a-conservation-canine-handler-do-you-have-what-it-takes/

Career profile, Louise Wilson: https://www.conservation-careers.com/career-stories/conservation-dogs/

Using Scent Detection Dogs in Conservation Settings: https://www.frontiersin.org/articles/10.3389/fvets.2016.00096/full

Wildlife Conservation Organizations

African Wildlife Foundation: https://www.awf.org/

Gorilla Doctors: https://www.gorilladoctors.org/

International Crane Foundation: https://www.savingcranes.org/

International Rhino Foundation: https://rhinos.org/

International Union for Conservation of Nature (IUCN): https://www.iucn.org/

The Nature Conservancy: https://www.nature.org/en-us/

Panthera: https://www.panthera.org/

Project Aware: https://www.projectaware.org/

Wildlife Alliance: https://www.wildlifealliance.org/

Wildlife Conservation Society: https://www.wcs.org/

World Wildlife Fund: https://www.worldwildlife.org/

6

Teaching Trainers without Turning Them Off

There are hurdles in teaching trainers, especially using the label "positive reinforcement" trainer and figuring out what that implies. Addressing the difficulty and the semantic arguments that surround the terms "positive reinforcement" and "punishment" have been at the center of my philosophy and my consulting work for many years. Following the first two articles in this chapter are general thoughts and guidelines for teaching people how to train better. As people get more comfortable with training principles, they begin to see training happening everywhere they look, as I experienced with a video game and movies.

Is It Really All or Nothing?

If I shared my travel schedule, most people would be horrified at how much time I spend on the road! A good amount of the consulting I do is with professional trainers and programs looking for a way to transition to using positive reinforcement methods. I have been working with many of these organizations for more than 10 years now, and a great deal of that work I have carried with me into my role with Karen Pryor Clicker Training.

Coincidence… ?

It has long been my mission to help more traditionally based trainers find useful solutions to the various training challenges they face by introducing them to positive reinforcement methodologies. Assisting people with a background in coercion-based training can be difficult, time-consuming, and filled with roadblocks. But, when we make breakthroughs and I see trainers use new tools and be successful with those new tools, it is rewarding and reinforcing for me! This is an area where I feel I can make a significant difference; my work over the past decade has convinced me it is worth the effort.

In a span of just a few weeks, I worked with five different groups that included several law enforcement agencies, a service-dog organization, a guide-dog organization, and a group of serious dog-sports enthusiasts. As usual, each group had its own unique challenges and obstacles—and each stretched my training abilities in new ways. These varying needs and issues can be frustrating and exciting at the same time.

I wanted to share an obstacle that I faced on three separate occasions, an obstacle that came from an unexpected place. While each of the three conversations I had were different and sprung from completely different sources, they each presented an obstacle that was eerily similar. All of the encounters were private conversations that I had with individuals during the time I was working with their organization or group. I will detail one specific conversation for the purposes of this discussion.

Client: "I appreciate the knowledge you bring to us, Ken, but I can't drink the Kool-Aid! I can't really become a positive reinforcement trainer!"

Ken: "Why not? I am not trying to make you drink some artificial potion!" (I feel myself getting defensive, so I pull back my intensity and continue in a more calming voice.) "In fact, there is nothing hidden in what I am sharing with you. I am simply teaching various scientific principles and practical tools that will help you become a better trainer and improve your program. I want to give you new options for dealing with problem behavior so that you get better results!"

Client: "But some of the tools don't make sense for my needs," he says in a rather snippy tone.

Ken: "I know! That's why I am giving you lots of options, so that you can use the tools that are most appropriate for you and your style of training. Choose the tool or application that you understand and that makes sense for whatever particular challenge you face. I will help you apply the techniques effectively, over time."

Client: "But I was told that if I don't embrace the entire philosophy, then it is pointless to use just a few of the techniques. Mixing and matching coercion with positive reinforcement dilutes the effectiveness of both tools! And I am not ready to completely throw out my 25 years of training experience for a new fad!"

Ken: "Whoa, whoa, whoa! Hold on a minute! Let me figure out what you're trying to say. Where did you hear this? I think you have some misconceptions about positive reinforcement. What I am hoping to teach you is certainly not a fad nor is it new. Can you explain why you feel this way?"

Client: "I thought I would try to get a head start on understanding positive reinforcement by taking classes from a private trainer and using the techniques with my dogs at home. So, I signed up for a class and was told by the instructor that she would not work with me. If I wanted to learn about positive reinforcement, it was all or nothing. I could not use any corrections or it would negate all the work that we would accomplish using positive reinforcement. The instructor was pretty snooty about it and copped a serious attitude with me. So, I said 'forget that!' I have well-behaved dogs already; I don't really need her class."

Ken: "Do me a favor. Give me a chance this week and if you don't see a way that I can help you, we can say goodbye and you don't have to talk to me about positive reinforcement again! I think you may have misunderstood the instructor or caught her on a bad day, but let me clear up a few things for you..."

I won't go further with this particular dialogue but will simply say that this individual changed his point of view by the end of the week. He is looking forward to having me back to work with his organization again later in the year! If the conversation above had been my only conversation of that type, I probably would not be sharing this story. But I am sharing it because I had three similar conversations. Each conversation had slightly different specifics, but the people I spoke with all told me that they had reached out to or talked to another positive reinforcement trainer and were turned off to the use of positive reinforcement because of that conversation.

I had been on the road traveling for a few weeks in a row, but instead of being excited by the progress I had made at each organization and feeling happy to be headed home, I was troubled the entire flight home. All I could think about was that my biggest obstacle at each location had been conversations my clients had with other positive reinforcement trainers. Are we sabotaging our own cause without realizing it?

My must-solve issues

I am hopeful that these three incidents were just isolated and unique coincidences. I know many colleagues who share my philosophy and hope, so I find comfort in that fact. However, I also felt it was important to share this experience with readers, to share my initial thoughts on the topics that this experience raised for me. Here are the key issues for me:

1. Working with traditional trainers and determining how best to help them transition to the use of positive reinforcement
2. Talking with trainers whose approach differs from our own, using positive reinforcement ourselves
3. Defining what it really means to be a positive-reinforcement-based trainer
4. Misunderstanding the terms "punishment" and "reinforcement" and how our effort to teach science-based concepts collides with the general public's understanding of these terms
5. Addressing the challenges of teaching broad, general concepts and applying rules to the use of concepts that apply to all scenarios

As you can see, this experience opened up a wide spectrum of thoughts. I want to share and discuss the first two in detail. The next three I'll address in the next piece, "Taking a More Nuanced Approach to the Terms 'Reinforcement' and 'Punishment.'"

Positive options in a real world

The first two issues in my list apply to working with trainers who use coercive techniques regularly—the type of clients I worked with during my recent weeks of travel. I think the "all or nothing" philosophy comes from a well-intentioned place, but it is unrealistic to maintain that philosophy dealing with trainers who already have a history of using aversive control and correction-based tools. There are options for handling the following obstacles these trainers present.

Mixing reinforcers and punishers in the same learning environment

The real world is filled with reinforcers and punishers; they are around us all the time. We, along with our animals, learn from these experiences every day. The existence of both reinforcers and punishers in our world does not by their very presence negate their effectiveness. We can recognize that a stovetop allows us to cook a delicious and reinforcing meal and also learn that touching the stovetop's hot surface with a bare hand is painful. Our long-term lessons about being around a stove will depend on the context and history of our collective experiences around that kitchen appliance. If every time we try to cook that delicious meal we always end up touching the stove and burning a hand, that experience (due to our clumsiness, ineptness, or inappropriate tool use) may teach us that the meal we crave simply is not worth it.

But if taught to cook properly, with the right tools, we may avoid or reduce the chances of getting burned again. Our comfort level using a stove and cooking our favorite meal will become more powerful than the rare times we are burned. Thus, we'll still be eager to cook that meal. My point is that punishers and reinforcers work in our environment side by side all the time. However, as positive reinforcement trainers, we recognize that the use of punishers, or any aversive, can break down the trust and relationship we have worked so hard to develop with our animals. This is one of the reasons we don't recommend mixing the two. Working with young or new trainers, we can teach them how to use positive reinforcement in a way that eliminates the need to introduce any corrections at all. But that is not the case if we are trying to help a traditionally trained trainer transition to the use of positive reinforcement.

Using aversive control around animals that have never experienced it, or haven't experienced it in many years.

It is understandable that some trainers may want to prevent other learners in the classroom (animals and people) from being exposed to corrections if those learners have not seen or experienced corrections before. That exposure can be a very upsetting and uncomfortable experience. This may be a valid reason for not wanting someone who uses corrections instinctively to be in a classroom setting. However, there are several options available besides simply denying the person access to classroom instruction. One option is to explain why you would like him or her to avoid using those tools in your classroom. Many trainers and owners are more than willing to try—as long as you set clear expectations and help them through the challenges they will face for the first class or two.

Another option is to offer a separate class (or a private class) to a handler who has a history of using correction techniques. This alternative prevents other students from being impacted by the use of aversive tools. You may find, as I have, that it only takes one or two classes for a handler to gain enough discipline to avoid using old standby tools in a classroom setting. After starting with private classes, the handler can join a larger class. If we want to see coercion-based trainers make the transition, we need to find a way to work with them.

Step by step

My experiences over the years have helped me recognize that it takes time for someone who has used a skill or technique for many years to change to a new method or to use new tools. Just as we teach behavior to our animals in small steps, successive approximations, I have found that teaching trainers to move away from the use of corrections requires the appropriate steps and an adequate amount of time. We have to help these learners by setting them up for success. Give them steps and goals that are achievable and reachable, and move them toward the goal of using positive reinforcement in small increments.

If we are successful trainers, this is a process we have already used hundreds of times with animals. Why not use it with human learners as well? Successive approximation is the only method that I have used successfully as a consultant. There will be no change or progress if I come in and suggest that the client must stop doing everything that has worked for the past 30 years! I cannot, and do not, expect coercion-based trainers to leave all the tools they know behind and switch to a new set of tools all at once. Instead, I need to assess their needs and make the transition slowly one or two tools at a time.

This training process has to be executed thoughtfully so that the client can be successful in the transition. If we expect a client who wants to learn to use positive reinforcement to make the transition all at once, we are making the task far too difficult. Seeing success will be the most reinforcing event and will lead the client to want to use more new tools. If I introduce the transition correctly, the client will often be eager to move even more quickly than I will allow. As much as I want eager clients to use the new tools, sometimes I am forced to slow down the pace to build a solid foundation before adding more layers.

Positive reinforcement: offered to all!

A concern that has plagued me for years is that some positive reinforcement trainers fail to use the techniques they use so well with their animals when they are working with their human clients. I appreciate the passion with which we hold to our conviction that positive reinforcement is an effective and more humane approach to use when training animals. But sometimes that heartfelt emotion clouds our approach to talking about the science logically. More often than not, that approach makes our passion seem like harsh criticism of anyone who doesn't train the same way we do. I fear that some who profess to embrace positive reinforcement forget that, unless they are grounded in the science and use positive reinforcement with the people around them, they will fail to make an effective case and fail to convert anyone.

In each training environment that I worked in during the busy travel time I've described, the people with whom I worked reported that they were turned away from positive reinforcement not because of the science or practical elements of its application but because of the attitude of the trainer who tried to convert them initially. This is not the first report of this news, but it alarmed me to face that obstacle three times in the span of just a few weeks. I know many positive reinforcement trainers who are equally good at the application of reinforcement with the animals they train and the people they teach. Until we can all move in that direction, we will fail to convince those considering new tools to make the switch.

More to come

Obviously, this is an issue that is important to me. I desperately want to spread the science and application of positive reinforcement techniques to more people. We owe it to the animals that we care for to teach scientifically sound, practically effective, and humanely appropriate techniques to those who want to improve their training. But we need to make sure that we are not the very impediments that keep this from happening.

Taking a More Nuanced Approach to the Terms "Reinforcement" and "Punishment"

In my piece titled "Is it Really All or Nothing?" (p. 138), I described a few of my concerns about the obstacles some positive reinforcement trainers place in the way of converting new trainers to positive techniques. Sometimes we are our own worst enemies in helping new trainers embrace positive reinforcement. There were two main topics I focused on in that article. The first was the reluctance many trainers feel in allowing more traditional trainers to convert to the use of positive reinforcement tools gradually. The other issue that I addressed was the troubling trend of being overly critical, and not very positive, in the approach that some take talking about or to trainers who have not yet adopted positive reinforcement.

Those two topics will continue to be important issues for our community, but this article will focus on how the terminology we use often gets in the way of conveying the desired message. Interestingly, after the "Is it Really All or Nothing?" article came out, many people forwarded articles, blogs, and essays that others had written about the topic of punishment and reinforcement—and the confusion that exists about these concepts in training circles. I would like to add my voice and explanation to this conversation.

"Purely positive?"

Phrases that will raise a skeptical eye or turn others off to our message quickly are comments such as, "I am a purely positive trainer," or "I never use punishment!" I appreciate the sentiment behind these statements, but it is easy to understand why some scoff at those comments and assume that anyone who makes those statements is not a serious trainer. I don't think those assumptions are necessarily true, but it highlights the challenges and obstacles that the use of terminology creates.

To whom are we speaking?

Perhaps one of the first challenges is not knowing or understanding the background either of the person delivering a particular message or of the person receiving the message. When those involved in a conversation are from different backgrounds, there is often a huge difference in the terms each of them uses and understands. Professional trainers often focus on vastly different approaches to their craft: operant conditioning, classical conditioning, ethology, several new Eastern philosophies, and traditional mentorships (that may or may not have a grounding in one of the previously mentioned approaches). In addition to communicating with professional trainers, we must find ways of communicating with the general public—people who may have little understanding of technical terminology. Even professional trainers, depending on their background, may use vastly different terms. Word choice and vocabulary are often at the crux of a communication breakdown.

I approach training in an operant way and, while I certainly use knowledge of classical conditioning and ethology, my terminology and toolset come from the operant part of the science. When I communicate with the public, however, I revert to language and terms that are more commonly understood. This choice can be confusing if you are not aware that I change languages depending on my intended audience. If we want to have an honest dialogue about techniques, we have to recognize that we may each be bringing a different understanding of terms and concepts to the table.

Reinforcers and punishers are always at work on behavior

The phrase "purely positive" is neither realistic nor truthful. I have never used that term and can't even imagine what that phrase really means. Both pleasing and aversive stimuli are around us all the time, and the frequencies of various behaviors in an animal's repertoire are constantly in flux. As those behaviors change in frequency, they are, by definition, being reinforced or punished. Reinforcement and punishment are occurring every day to every animal, no matter what type of trainer we claim to be. If we understand the science, we know this to be true. The truth requires that skilled trainers recognize and understand how to use all the tools, and how to adapt the environment to set up animals for success.

So, what do the various labels that we put on trainers really mean? I will not presume to speak for anyone other than myself. But I can explain why I call myself a positive reinforcement trainer and what that means to me.

Explaining training to the general public

I have spent a great deal of my career talking about training to the layman, or the non-trainer. Even many of the young trainers I have worked with did not come from a science background and often were unfamiliar with the technical terminology. As a result, I talk about punishment and reinforcement the way the public understands it quite frequently.

In our society we tend to punish and reinforce *people, children, and animals.* But if you are a true trainer, you never punish or reinforce *a person or an animal*; you punish or reinforce *behavior*. This is a concept that is lost on the average person, someone who does not have the time, interest, or inclination to understand that distinction. We see it all the time: people punish their dog, punish their child, or punish the criminal. Sadly, this punishment often does not yield the desired result, yet we continue to punish in our society.

Gradually, I have come to realize that we need to make a greater effort to help the average person really understand the science of training in order to help make the interactions with their pets and the people in their lives more successful. But unless I am planning to teach that "science lesson" specifically, if I am communicating with a broad, non-scientific audience, I may make the statement that "I never use punishment." In that instance I mean punishment as the general public understands and uses that word. I am not referring to the behavioral definition of punishment.

Teaching training to young trainers

I have taught hundreds, perhaps thousands, of young trainers on the path to becoming professional trainers. I have taught them in environments where I could dictate what tools they were allowed to use and when they were allowed to use them. With these students, I do teach the real meaning of reinforcement and punishment. It is important to me that they are aware of how the environment reinforces and punishes behavior, and how they should adapt their actions to compensate for that. As a result of the controlled environment, and because I am able to ensure that they are not working with animals that have serious behavior problems, I can insist that the student focus on positive reinforcement, and forbid the purposeful application of any punishers.

If an animal presents problems, my student trainers are encouraged to redirect toward more appropriate behavior or to pass the animal to a more experienced trainer, someone with the option to use a broader tool set. During these formative learning years, this approach to punishment teaches young trainers how to use reinforcement effectively. Since punishment is not available to them, they learn to find positive alternatives. These students become far more disciplined trainers who, later in their careers, when the option to use punishment tools is opened up to them, do not find it easy or necessary to use those tools. Using positive options first becomes second nature; punishment options are simply not the default response for trainers schooled in this system. These trainers, during the early years of their training, truly are using only positive reinforcement.

Working with clients

Most clients have even fewer skills and less knowledge than the young trainers I described. Usually I teach clients only the tools they need to work effectively with their particular pets in their specific environment. I find that the positive tools are quite effective for beginners; focusing on those tools prevents an overly emotional use of a punisher because I avoid teaching clients those tools at all. In severe cases, where some aversive tool might be selected traditionally, I suggest the client seek out a professional trainer (me or someone else) who can guide them in the safe and appropriate use of a more advanced tool. I avoid putting those tools in the clients' hands. I find it too easy for beginners to overuse punishment or escalate it to a level that is so harsh that it does serious damage to the learner. It takes a much higher skill level than the average client possesses to apply punishers appropriately.

My approach to professionals

When I am working with professional colleagues, labeling myself as a positive reinforcement trainer indicates that I focus my attention on promoting/increasing desired behavior as opposed to reducing/eliminating unwanted behavior. I look for ways to reinforce desired behavior instead of focusing attention on getting rid of unwanted behavior. I acknowledge that if one behavior is increasing in frequency, there is likely another behavior that is decreasing at the same time.

Looking at behavior that way, reinforcement and punishment are, by default, occurring all the time for every trainer in all learning situations. However, my concern or attention is on what my learners are experiencing. Where is their focus? If they are performing a behavior out of fear or concern for getting it wrong—or are avoiding an aversive—I have failed in my goals as a positive reinforcement trainer.

I am hopeful that my animal is seeking to get it right and is working for the joy, thrill, or reinforcement of the activity. My approach can be equated to the various ways human workers look at their jobs. Some work hard and are motivated by the fear of losing their job or fear of getting in trouble; these people work hard, do excellent work, but have a poor attitude and hate their jobs. There are other workers (and I consider myself one of them) who never think about getting fired and are not motivated by fear; instead we do our work well, enjoy our jobs, and are motivated by the reinforcement that we get for that work (joy of the job, mission, coworkers, and, almost secondarily, a paycheck).

There are a few positive reinforcement trainers who refuse to acknowledge that punishers are operating on their animals at all. But I think that group is small and not the norm. Most of us who consider ourselves positive reinforcement trainers are neither ignorant of nor oblivious to the realities of punishment. We are keenly conscious of the impact that aversives have on animals, and use that knowledge with skill and care. Punishers are certainly part of the learning and teaching that takes place in all training programs—but they don't have to be the focus, and they certainly don't need to be the most prominent for the animal that is learning.

My way of thinking about reinforcement and punishment comes from a desire to teach with clarity and set an ethical standard and a guideline for myself, my staff, my clients, and my students. I believe in the science and try to teach the science with clarity and objectivity. I share this information with the hope that it clarifies my approach and reasons for calling myself a positive reinforcement trainer; I make no judgment or criticism of those who choose to train or teach differently.

The dialogue continues

As our profession grows and our use and understanding of the science expands, I hope we can discover similarities among us and lessons we can learn from each other, no matter what label we put on our style of training. The goal of this piece was simply to share why I use the term "positive reinforcement training" and why I avoid or minimize punishment when I train or describe my training. It is my ongoing desire to bridge the huge gap that still exists between many of us who train animals as professionals, and to help us continue learning from each other.

Recipes, Rules, and Principles

As a lecturer and coach, my ultimate goal is to teach principles, rather than "recipes" and rules. A solid understanding of principles allows students to solve a wide variety of problems independently, but I have found that offering recipes, suggesting rules, and imparting principles all have their place in developing skilled trainers.

The starting block

I am amazed how often students come in with levels of understanding that fall on opposite ends of the learning spectrum. Some students understand learning theory but are at a loss when it is time to apply the principles to an animal in front of them. These students need some rules or recipes to get them started successfully. Other students have learned to follow a recipe but seem unable to recognize when to break the rules to respond to an animal's needs. These students need a better grasp of the big picture and of the guiding principles of learning. The best students are those that come in with an understanding of both, but I find that those students are rare!

Acknowledge the audience

Sometimes the right approach depends on how much time I am able to spend with my learners. I approach students in a weekend seminar differently, for example, than I approach a long-term client or employee.

When I oversaw staff at the Shedd Aquarium in Chicago, I helped each trainer progress through an early set of rules, and adjusted those rules as each individual gained experience. Over a period of several years, I shaped my novice trainers into advanced trainers who understood the overriding principles of training.

When I teach a class or seminar, on the other hand, I may never see the students again. They walk away with whatever information I give them. I do my best to give them enough information to be useful right away when they get home while also providing a broader framework so that they can be successful in the future as their training skills progress.

Rules: a boost, but never a crutch

I have come to appreciate the value of training recipes or sets of rules; sometimes they are the steps necessary to lead a novice trainer toward a better understanding of complex concepts. Guidelines such as "Don't keep your hand in your pouch," "Every click must be followed by a treat," or "Use a cue only once—don't repeat it" help inexperienced trainers make better choices. Many of these rules assist in developing trainers' mechanical skills while they learn to train, but as trainers gain experience, these skills become automatic or second nature. When a trainer no longer has to focus on these rules, it frees up brain space to concentrate on next training steps, distractions, and reading the animal's body language. As students gain experience and learn to interpret the behavior of their animals, they begin to understand the reasons for the rules, but they also recognize that these "rules" are only guidelines.

As teachers, it is important to ensure that students are not allowed to get stuck on a set of rules for too long because that can prevent them from progressing. Recently, I was working with a student who realized that she needed to re-cue a behavior to set her dog up for success, but she hesitated. She asked, "Isn't it a sin to repeat a cue?" Her question allowed me to explain why that rule was probably given to her; it also provided an opening to discuss both the merits and the limitations of that rule. My student was relieved, but the incident made me keenly aware of the need to give students and clients more information.

When I am teaching a hands-on course at The Ranch or working with a client, it is rare that I am not faced with rule conflicts that stymie the less-experienced trainer. For example, the trainer is working with her dog, the dog does not do the cued behavior, but the trainer accidentally clicked. What should she do? One rule says, "Follow every click with a treat." Another rule says, "Don't reinforce behavior that you don't want." My answer is, "It depends." You want to do what will help give the animal the most clarity and cause the least confusion. My recommendation is to be more careful when you click. I might even suggest a new rule: "When in doubt, don't click." If you realize a few moments later that the behavior was worth reinforcing, you can still reinforce. But, back to the question of what to do in that moment. In most cases I would not reinforce, since I do not want to reinforce unwanted behavior. The one exception might be if this session was one of the first introductions to the clicker, but even then I would probably not reinforce. An adverse learning experience is only likely to occur if the trainer makes that mistake more than once. If that starts to happen, the trainer is not ready to use a clicker.

Beyond rules and recipes

The word "recipe" brings to mind an analogy. I am far from being a chef. When I try to cook a particular dish for the first time, I need to follow a recipe so that I can create a reasonably palatable meal. As I gain confidence with the utensils and ingredients, I can begin to experiment with flavors and vary ingredients with good results. But I also find that if I fail to understand certain principles of cooking, I can vary too much, and the resulting mess is inedible. As a beginner, the recipe is an excellent guide, but the experienced chef is guided by broader principles that allow him or her to create great meals.

Rules and recipes can get learners on the right path more quickly, but we need to give learners the information and ability to move beyond those rules as they gain experience. I still don't have the perfect solution for imparting principles to my students and clients successfully. The realization that recipes and rules are part of the process has been a significant step in getting me closer to that goal.

The Good-to-Great Trainer Transformation: How to Get There

Trainers never set out to be merely adequate. We want to be good trainers. Many of the trainers I meet go to ClickerExpo and attend seminars with the hope of improving their training. Their goals are to become the best trainers they can be. It's not unusual to hear someone ask, *"How can I transition from being a good trainer to being a great trainer?"*

For more than 25 years, I was on the leadership team at the Shedd Aquarium in Chicago. Our CEO, Ted, asked us to read the book *Good to Great: Why Some Companies Make the Leap… and Others Don't* by Jim Collins. It is a business book that examines the progress of 1,435 good companies over the course of 40 years. The author then looks at the 11 companies that transformed from good to great companies. What did these high-performance companies have in common?

The connection between the corporate world and an education-and-conservation-based organization was not immediately clear to me and my colleagues. Quietly and patiently, Ted allowed us to discover the connection and helped us realize that the pathways to success and greatness were similar no matter what the venture. We learned that none of the "great" companies had followed a specific program or prescription for success, but they did have qualities in common.

Recently, I revisited the success factors that Collins discovered in his research to see if there was any application to the training world. Could the areas of focus that propelled companies from good to great be helpful to trainers?

The egg

Jim Collins wrote about many companies whose accomplishments are perceived by the outside world as overnight successes or miraculous transformations. But Collins found that, for truly great companies, that is never the case. He described the process as like an egg that lies dormant. To the uninformed, the egg may appear unimpressive and not particularly notable—until the chick pops out and, suddenly, there is a living bird! It may be a miracle of nature, but it is hardly an overnight or unpredictable success. The bird did not suddenly appear. There was an incubation and formative period that, while not observable to the outsider, was taking place long before the actual hatching. Similarly, great companies don't just become great suddenly; they work hard to get there.

The same holds true for becoming a great trainer—there are no shortcuts. It takes hard work and practice. Attending a conference or a seminar gives you new information and can help expand your thinking about training, but improving your skills requires a lifelong dedication to learning, practicing, and adjusting your actions until you get better. When you do get better, you will be the first to acknowledge that it was neither quick nor miraculous, and that you worked your tail off to reach that goal!

The flywheel effect

A flywheel is a giant, heavy, metal wheel on an axis that spins when it gathers enough momentum. Collins' analysis looks at the company as a flywheel; for a company to succeed it must get the flywheel spinning. If the flywheel is not in motion, it takes a great deal of effort to push on the wheel and get it moving. As the wheel begins to turn, it gains momentum and becomes easier and easier to push and keep going.

Many companies stagnate and don't keep up with trends or changing business situations. A business must "get the flywheel turning" by accepting change and implementing needed adjustments. At first that takes effort, and it requires a culture of change and an awareness of the world outside the walls of the company.

Trainers also need to be open to change. We must keep up with scientific advances, new literature and thoughts on welfare, and improved techniques for using tools and practicing our skills. It is so easy to get into a routine and not adapt or grow. As I look at my own training flywheel, I find that I have to work hard to accept and implement change.

The Flywheel Training Cycle:

- Learn a new skill or concept
- Apply and practice the skill or concept

- Evaluate its effectiveness (rely on colleagues or coworkers to help when possible)
- Adjust based on feedback
- Repeat

Disciplined thought: fox or hedgehog?

Collins bases the idea of disciplined thought on a Greek parable that "distinguishes between foxes, which know many small things, and hedgehogs, which know one big thing." His research revealed that every great company had leaders who were hedgehogs, people who were able to simplify complex concepts and ideas into a single unifying vision. Hedgehog-led companies did not try to be good at all things; instead, they paid attention to their core values, which guided all decision-making.

To be great trainers, we each have to discover our personal "hedgehog." What is our niche? Which skills are our best skills? Where should we focus attention? My "hedgehog" can be articulated as "I am a positive-reinforcement trainer who puts the animal's needs first and teaches others how to be the best trainers they can be through education and skill-development." I may do more things than that, but it is the essence of what I believe in and it guides my decision-making about all projects. If a project does not fit into my area of focus, I will likely recommend a different consultant or trainer.

Your hedgehog may be very different; it should be uniquely your own. The following are some examples of different types of personal or organizational hedgehogs:

- I specialize in puppy training and assisting clients as they get their relationships off to the best start possible, focusing on positive reinforcement and thorough client education.
- We deal with all things agility, providing instruction and classes for all agility enthusiasts from the beginner to the advanced, serious competitor.
- We are problem-solving consultants specializing in reactivity and aggression issues. We help find the root cause of behavioral problems and look for lasting positive solutions for clients and their dogs.

Everyone's hedgehog is personal. It is where you want to focus all of your primary effort and energy. It is ultimately what you do best and what you want to do better; it is where you want to dedicate the maximum resources.

The bus

One of the last important principles discovered in the good-to-great research is that leaders of great companies are the drivers of a philosophical bus, driving their organizations toward success. They let everyone know where they are headed, and they are careful about whom they let on the bus. Great leaders will also move people to the appropriate seats on the bus; they do not allow employees to stay in positions they are not well-suited for.

Trainers should not take on projects or training tasks that they are not suited for or skilled enough to train. In determining what we want to train, we should make sure the skill or task is suited to our animal. Ensure that the learner is "in the right seat on the bus." Too often I see trainers determined to teach a dog to be an agility competitor, but the dog does not enjoy it and does not have a temperament suited to this high-energy sport. The great trainer will recognize the mismatch, decide to find other things for that dog to do, and avoid forcing the dog into an ill-fitting activity. The best trainers develop a program and a plan that matches the animal's skill set and interest level.

The path to excellence

No matter what we do, pathways to excellence are similar. There is no substitute for the tried-and-true methods of hard work, education, practice, evaluation, and adjustment. We must know our own strengths and those of our learners, and focus our energies on the things that matter most to us.

I may never achieve greatness as a trainer, but that has never been my goal. The day that I stop learning, growing, and improving is the day I should retire. The pursuit of excellence in training should be focused on improving the lives of the animals we care about, and the pursuit must start with improving our own knowledge and skills. The quest for improvement is never-ending. It is a journey that we share with the people and pets in our lives. It is a collaboration that will not occur just because we wish it or want it so. To achieve lasting and impactful excellence, we must dedicate the resources, mind-power, and effort in a conscious and deliberate way.

References

Collins, J. (2001). *Good to Great: Why Some Companies Make the Leap... and Others Don't*. Harper-Collins, New York, NY.

Training Lessons from Pokémon Go

I am a behavior geek. I see the laws of behavior in everyday activities because that's how I've learned to see the world. I appreciate well-thought-out, deliberate uses of behavior analysis principles. Recently, I have enjoyed experiencing the power of positive reinforcement in the immensely popular game Pokémon Go.

I don't normally play video games, except for a brief fascination with Ms. Pacman more than 30 years ago. But as the Pokémon craze was taking off, a good friend and colleague began playing the game. I remember her commenting on the brilliant use of reinforcement in the game and suggesting to me, "You should play it, then write an article about it."

The game made headlines as the most downloaded app of 2016, so the idea intrigued me. I remember thinking, "I'll play it for a few weeks and see what all the fuss is about." Six months later, I'm still playing. The game uses reinforcement exceptionally well! I wanted to share a few observations.

A simplified explanation

It turns out I am still learning and discovering new aspects of the Pokémon Go game, and I don't want to bore non-players with too many details, so I'll give a basic explanation (apologies to the die-hard fans). The game was designed to get players out of their homes by encouraging them to be active—to walk and explore the world around them. The premise of the game is that the world is inhabited by many fascinating creatures called Pokémon (affectionately called Pokeys by some fans). The player's goal is to catch every kind of Pokey, advance to higher levels, and control "gyms," battle arenas that earn the player coins that can be used to purchase useful items. The game is tied to the player's GPS. As a virtual version of the player walks around the neighborhood, Pokeys appear. The player throws balls at the Pokeys to catch them.

Good use of behavior principles

I see people of all ages playing this game on their phones everywhere I go: airports, department stores, restaurants, and public parks. Players seem addicted to Pokémon Go. Why is the game so popular? I think the answer is the game's great application of key behavior principles. It uses frequent reinforcement, a variety of reinforcement types, and novel ways of earning reinforcement. Reinforcers come in the form of points, candy, stardust, coins, advancement to new levels, acquisition of new tools for the game, opportunities to evolve your Pokeys into more advanced creatures, and the ability to win battles against other Pokeys in gyms. The game is well-designed to keep players wanting more; it's an addictive pastime. I couldn't help but think about how we want our learners to have a similar experience, and a desire to keep playing (training).

The learning experience

I did not expect the game to help me look at training from new perspectives, but I had two revelations playing the game that I think make it a great learning tool for trainers. The first of these revelations was watching the phenomena of behavior principles unfold. I felt powerless to overcome them or change them. The second revelation was experiencing learning without verbal instruction, something our animals deal with every day.

Behavior phenomena

In addition to the great application of reinforcement already described, I witnessed the power of learning in action, which gave me insights into what animals may experience when they train with us.

- *Superstitious behavior:* Because there is little written instruction for Pokémon Go, I learned the game through trial and error. I developed patterns of behavior that I was sure were critical, but they turned out to be irrelevant to the outcome. These patterns included holding my phone at just the right angle to catch Pokeys and touching certain items on the screen thinking that would allow me to move on to the next activity. For example, originally I tapped the bubbles that appeared after swiping a Poké stop* because I thought that was the only way to collect the items it produced. In fact, tapping was unnecessary. When I tapped the bubbles, they burst in a satisfying manner and I received items, which "trained" me to be a great bubble-burster. I was so surprised to find out that this was just superstitious behavior.

I learned that other players had developed the habit of shaking their phones to keep the Pokeys contained or counting out loud the number of seconds before a Pokey was caught; these were more superstitious behaviors. I realized just how easily unnecessary actions are reinforced. For months I was certain that each action was needed for success before it was pointed out to me that they all had no impact on the game's outcome. How often have I seen that in animals?

- *Resurgence:* Once I discovered that certain actions were not needed, I quit doing them and changed my habits. But, if I was focusing on something new or distracted by some other activity, those previously learned superstitious behaviors came surging back. I felt incapable of stopping myself from doing them. My finger reached to pop the bubbles before I was conscious of it doing so.

  I've seen this phenomenon often in an animal I was training and thought to myself, "He knows better!" However, resurgence has nothing to do with knowing better; an animal just reverts to a behavior that had previously been so reinforcing. It was fascinating to see how the game brought that behavior out in me.

Non-verbal learning

As I mentioned, the game app offers little in the way of instruction. I suppose I could have gone online and searched for videos and articles that explain secrets of the game, but I never bothered to do so. From time to time, I checked with my friend who taught me elements of the game that I had not yet discovered or pointed out misconceptions about what I thought I knew about the game.

The experience of learning the game without explicit instructions gave me a greater appreciation for how the animals I train must feel when I don't provide clear information. Overall, the game is well designed, and I was learning how to play through carefully planned experiences. Learning the game made me appreciate that properly applied behavioral principles can provide clear information to the learner. Imagine how much better we should be as trainers, since we have the power to see and interpret animals' responses in real time! We are able to react with carefully applied behavior principles, leading to even more powerful communication with our learners.

Implications

I couldn't help but ponder the greater implications that this game presented. If we could arrange reinforcers in the real world the way that game designers do, imagine how much better life would be. There are many successful teachers, coaches, parents, and trainers who do just that; they arrange the environment carefully in ways that set their learners up for success. They create environments rich with reinforcers of many types. But the reinforcers cannot just be arbitrarily available in these scenarios; to be successful, we must make sure the reinforcers are paired with desired behavior in a timely way.

There were many lessons that became clear as I played Pokémon Go. Many are training principles that we all use every day. We need to keep searching for ways to apply them. B.F. Skinner wrote, "What is wrong with life in the West is not that it has too many reinforcers, but that the reinforcers are not contingent upon the kinds of behavior that sustain the individual or promote survival of the culture or species." These are powerful words that I hope we can all take to heart. There are so many valuable lessons that trainers can take from the world around them, even from the imaginary world of a video game.

Note

*Poké stops are real-world locations where players can collect items to help them in the game. They are all over every city and might be a statue in a park, a train station, the local library, a water tower, or a well-known building. Since the game is tied to a player's GPS, you can only collect these virtual items when you are within a few feet of the Poké stop.

Training Lessons from Summer Movies

I love talking, teaching, learning, and participating in training activities. Another great passion of mine is film. I see an average of three movies in the theater a week—if not more. I seem to find training lessons in every film I see, and I walk away with new pearls of training wisdom or fresh insights into behavior.

Three films stood out for me in the summer of 2015. One was a lesser-known film, titled *Max*, about a military dog and his recovery after the loss of his handler during an incident in Afghanistan. The other two films became the top two blockbuster films of the summer: *Jurassic World* and Disney Pixar's *Inside Out*.

Jurassic World and the clicker!

Jurassic World, the newest installment in the popular Jurassic Park series, is the type of film that summer blockbusters aspire to be. The movie is full of action, special effects, and a not-too-complicated plot: evil or greedy humans get their comeuppance at the hands of genetically engineered dinosaurs.

The protagonist, Owen Grady, played by Chris Pratt, is a dinosaur expert and trainer. That's right, he has built a relationship with four dangerous velociraptors, and the story revolves around that relationship and the training that Owen has accomplished with them. I enjoyed the film and really didn't think much about it afterward, until a few weeks later when so many colleagues were up in arms that Owen, the dinosaur trainer, used a clicker—and used it incorrectly! I watched the film a second time to see if I had missed something. The character Owen does indeed use a clicker, which he clicks many times. The clicking sound has been referenced in previous Jurassic Park films as a velociraptor feeding or hunting call. So while he was indeed using a clicker, I did not feel Owen used it incorrectly, just differently from the way many of us use one.

What struck me most about this story was the value the filmmakers placed on the relationship between the trainer and the dinosaurs. As trainers, we know that this is a key element in what we do. Owen's character showed compassion and an interest in doing the best he could for the animals for which he was responsible. This is a noble role that most of us who care for and train animals share.

Max, the hero dog

If you did not catch *Max* within the first two weeks of its release, you may have missed it. It didn't stick around in theaters for long, since it could not compete with the higher-octane films that summer is known for. A look at the fan-film internet site Rotten Tomatoes reveals the way the film was received: 75% of the public reviewed the film favorably, while only 39% of film critics gave it good marks. Some critics panned the film because of a problematic story, poor acting, and an overly predictable ending. Some trainers expressed concerns about a few references to traditional training methods and beliefs.

Although the story may take some liberties with the way military dogs do their jobs, I found the representation of a working military dog to have merit. I have worked with several military dogs and have great respect for the work they do and the way they assist servicemen and servicewomen in the field. The way the film focused on the challenges that a family, including the dog Max, faced and how they dealt with the loss of a loved one was realistic, and it was a story worth telling.

The story takes some unusual and perhaps far-fetched twists, but results in a misunderstood dog and a troubled teenage boy forming a strong bond and teaching those around them some valuable lessons along the way. I was able to accept the storyline for what it was: a vehicle for sharing the challenges of military conflict, the healing of a dysfunctional family, and the value of a bond between a boy and his dog. I appreciated the focus on relationship-building and the need to give dogs (and people) second chances. I am a strong believer in second chances for both dogs and the people in our lives. The film reminded me of the many ways obstacles can be put in the way of second chances. It is always easier to give up and not put forth an effort to help others overcome their challenges; working with them is hard. This powerful reminder added to the emotional impact of the film.

Inside Out and the emotions in our minds

The inventive animated film *Inside Out* revolves around a young girl named Riley who lives happily in Minnesota until her parents decide to move to San Francisco, which upsets Riley's life. The story is told from inside Riley's head, from the perspective of the five emotions that rule her life: Joy, Fear, Anger, Disgust, and Sadness. Each of these emotions takes a turn running the control center in Riley's brain; the film uses creative ways to show how these emotions interact and balance each other to make decisions that impact Riley's life.

Briefly, we get to see inside the parents' brains and see their emotions at work, and in a humorous segment we get to see inside the brains of a few household pets. But the focus of the story is on Riley, which is where I will focus as well. Joy was the controlling and predominant emotion for Riley before the family's relocation. Then Joy gets lost (figuratively and literally), and the other emotions take over. As Joy tries to make her way back into Riley's life, Joy believes she needs to suppress Sadness in order to return to Riley. In the end, Joy recognizes that the other emotions play a valuable part in providing balance to Riley's life. Each emotion plays an important role, making Riley the complete person that she is. All of those seemingly conflicting emotions are critical to her survival.

What a great lesson for trainers to take away from a movie! Sometimes I think we work so hard to suppress and change the emotional responses in our animals that we set ourselves up for a nearly impossible task. I don't think we want to get rid of those negative emotions completely; we just want to channel them in more productive ways. Fear, disgust, anger, and sadness all have a role in our pets' lives, not just joy. The "bad" emotions evolved for a reason: to protect us from danger. As trainers, we must find ways to show our dogs (cats, horses, or any animal) how to change emotional responses to certain triggers, but not erase those deeply rooted feelings completely. That is a difficult balance to find, and it is one of the reasons why the world needs skilled professional trainers. Our focus on positive reinforcement is the key to our success. While we hope that training will be a joyful experience for our animals, we recognize that other emotions are equally as important.

Positively Human

We often face challenges transferring animal teaching and training skills to the larger world—to our bosses, organizations, colleagues, spouses, friends, and customers. Why? As skilled positive animal trainers, we have become good observers of animal behavior, and we know how to arrange antecedents to set up animals for success and deliver robust, well-timed reinforcement. However, working with animals *does not* require good verbal communication skills or the keen observation of human behavior. Yet so much of applying positive reinforcement principles to people *does* require both, as the articles in this chapter illustrate.

Positive Reinforcement with People: It's Not Hierarchical!

Few of us are particularly adept at using positive reinforcement with people, even if we do it well with animals. Frequently I help people solve challenges with their clients and co-workers, and I especially enjoy cases that involve "superiors" of all kinds: bosses, parents, or coaches. I am often told, "I'm not in charge; I don't have the power to make a change." It may seem as though positive reinforcement is hierarchical, and that you can only influence behavior if you are in charge or officially in control, but that is not so.

Using reinforcement up the ladder

I began practicing the use of positive reinforcement "up the ladder" at a young age. My track coaches in high school and college were harsh, and my first employers in the animal-training field could be considered abusive by today's standards. While I felt just as oppressed, badgered, bullied, and harassed as everyone else on the team, I discovered that I could improve my situation once I learned to understand and navigate my social environment better.

First, I came to realize that my bosses and coaches were not out to get me. They had their own problems and worries, and their behaviors were shaped by other employees before me, by their own bosses, and by their own experiences. They were doing their best.

Next, I paid close attention to what my coaches and bosses were most interested in, the things that were clearly important (reinforcing) to them. For one of my coaches, it was being on time for practice and being well-prepared for that day's activities. For another coach, it was being respectful and calling him "Sir." For one boss, it was making sure his own supervisor was impressed, and for another boss, it was saving money and coming in under budget. Many times I remember thinking, even before I understood positive reinforcement, that "this guy seems super interested in… (fill in the blank)."

Stumbling across a formula that works

An early incident that comes to mind was an experience I had in high school with my track coach—a man whose idea of training was to berate and shout at students continuously. One cold winter day, I happened to arrive early to track practice and read the day's workout routine, which the coach always posted on a blackboard in the gym. He had scheduled an outdoor workout that included a run with ankle weights. When it was time for the team to meet, I was already wearing my outdoor sweats and weights. The coach shouted at the latecomers, demanding to know why nobody had taken the time to read the plan and come prepared to work out. Four of us had clearly paid attention and were prepared, but he didn't acknowledge us. At first, I was disappointed, but at least he hadn't yelled at me directly! As the practice came to a close, I realized that the coach hadn't raised his voice at me at all during that entire day's workout. The coach was still critical about the things I needed to improve, but he was kinder and noticeably less harsh. I remember making a mental note, "I need to try this again." The strategy continued to work, and my relationship with the coach grew stronger. Track became more fun for me, I began to excel at the sport, and the coach personally helped me earn a scholarship to a prestigious university track program.

The training plan

I found myself dealing with similar problems throughout my career. With time, I developed a successful strategy that I was able to replicate. The formula I use for handling difficult bosses and authority figures is straightforward:

1. Find the things your boss finds reinforcing; this may take time and observation. Reinforcers might be: coming in under budget, timeliness, impressing his or her boss, publications, awards, public recognition, discussing the local sports team, his or her kids, and so on.
2. Look for the things your boss finds aversive or punishing; again, this may take some time and observation. Examine all of your interactions and the interactions your boss has with other staff members. Punishers might include: someone interrupting his or her lunch, silly or irrelevant questions, rambling e-mails, his or her authority being questioned, unreliability, and so on.
3. Identify instances in which you can alleviate an aversive or deliver a reinforcer throughout the day.
4. Ask yourself, "Considering my position, what do I have the power or ability to do, and what am I less likely to be able to do?"

5. Make a plan, wait for the right opportunities, and execute the plan. Don't force it; wait to let it happen naturally.
6. Mean it. Set out to have a genuinely open attitude, and trust that things will fall into place. If you are not sincere, your efforts to reinforce will backfire.

Note about aversives: Is it you?

Make sure that you are not the cause of the problem. Does your boss seem to get annoyed by you? Are you the recipient of his wrath regularly? Does everyone else on staff seem to receive better treatment than you do? If so, ask yourself why. If you are creating aversives for your boss, you must eliminate them before you can attempt to use reinforcers.

Applying the formula

A zoo trainer, someone I will refer to as Sherry, felt that her boss, Dave, seldom assigned her the best projects. She felt passed over and overlooked. She also felt that Dave was a bully who made terrible decisions that made no sense, that he always got defensive when she asked him questions, and that he never took the time to explain his decisions to her. I asked Sherry if she showed as much contempt for Dave when she interacted with him as she was demonstrating in describing the problem to me. I suggested that although Sherry simply wanted to understand Dave's policies, Dave likely perceived her as a troublemaker, always challenging his authority. Sherry and I looked for ways she could reframe her questions and avoid putting Dave on the defensive. At first, Sherry felt that she was being manipulative, and she worried that it would seem that she was "brown-nosing" or "kissing up to the boss." I explained that she was simply giving Dave what he was looking for: respect and courtesy. A co-worker might perceive her actions as insincere, but what mattered was how Sherry meant it—and how Dave perceived it and responded to it.

When a relationship is broken, both sides have the power to start over and demonstrate good will. Sadly, people's egos get them stuck at an impasse because they can't bring themselves to be nice to someone they dislike. It becomes a vicious cycle. If we want to see change, we have to take on the responsibility to make the first move.

Once Sherry had a less contentious relationship with Dave, she was poised to start finding behaviors to reinforce. One of the reinforcers that seemed to motivate Dave was praise and recognition from his own boss. One day, Dave's supervisor complimented Sherry on a particularly innovative enrichment device in the warthog exhibit. Sherry saw her opportunity and said, "Thanks so much, but it was Dave who really encouraged the team to create these types of enrichments." The statement was truthful, sincere, and it wasn't overly enthusiastic, which made it effective. Over the course of the next year, Sherry found other opportunities to bring Dave recognition from his supervisor. Dave became more cordial and more helpful, and Sherry realized that her long-term quest to change Dave's behavior was working. She began receiving better assignments and no longer felt overlooked.

Be sincere

Sherry's case is not unique. Over the years I've coached many trainers successfully in the use of positive reinforcement with the people in their lives. It is a process that takes time and careful thought, and it requires empathy and understanding of the other person's perspective and needs. It cannot be rushed and must be approached in a sincere manner.

The laws of learning apply across all species; we should not forget that this includes the human animal as well.

The Path to Better Teaching: A Revealing Surgeon's Symposium

Trainers are essentially teachers. Our learners are not just the animals we train; our learners are also our clients, students, employees, and colleagues. Most of us spend a great deal of time perfecting our animal-training knowledge and skills, but few of us focus on skills that relate to the human learners—often creating our biggest challenges. I recently spoke at a surgeon's symposium in New York City that highlighted the universality of these challenges.

The invitation to participate in the symposium came from Dr. Martin Levy, a practicing orthopedic surgeon at Montefiore Medical Center. Dr. Levy had teamed up with Karen Pryor and Theresa McKeon to explore using TAGteach principles to teach basic surgical skills to medical students, such as setting up surgical instruments, using various tools, and tying suture knots. TAG is an acronym for Teaching with Acoustical Guidance, and it is a technique that uses a clicker to teach physical skills to people. It has been used to teach golfers to develop a better swing, gymnasts to improve their use of a balance beam, children to tie their shoes, and now surgeons to learn specific surgical skills. The project increased the speed with which medical students learned the skills and increased their proficiency at those skills. You can read about this project in more depth in the article in the *Scientific American* listed below. The symposium brought nine speakers together to show doctors in the New York City area the history of positive reinforcement training, the science behind it, and the results of the project to date.

After the event, all of the speakers got together for a private meeting that had two main goals. The first was to figure out how best to convince the medical community to abandon their old-school methods and switch to positive teaching techniques. But, a more general goal was to identify what a good teacher must do in order to set the learner up for success.

Here are some of the requirements we identified during that post-symposium meeting:

1. *Know the science and tools well.* Stay current with new scientific breakthroughs, and master the new skills.

2. *There are different types of learners, so adapt your teaching style accordingly*. For example, new medical students are part of the generation referred to as millennials. Some research indicates that this generation has a shorter attention span, thinks independently, and is accustomed to learning through electronic media.
3. *Break skills into the smallest possible components*. The learner can then master each of the smaller tasks that make up the larger, finished procedure. A surgeon must learn to use each tool and become proficient in handling and using those tools. Only after learning each individual skill can he or she put together the whole sequence successfully.
4. *Achieve fluency at each skill*. Fluency is about achieving mastery or proficiency at a task, and that includes accuracy, speed, quality, and pace, among other things. It is important to "over practice" each skill so that it becomes second nature. Fluency is so important in the teaching process because it allows the learner to go from success to success, with few or no mistakes. Fluency is fun!
5. *Use peer coaching*. In most disciplines, eventually learners need to pass on what they have learned to others. Just because a medical student has learned a skill proficiently doesn't mean he or she can teach others. The learning process needs to include the student learning to coach and help fellow students, and coaching ability consists of a different skill set. The surgical program at Montefiore Medical Center included peer-coaching in the learning process from the very start.
6. *Collect and interpret your data*. You need quantifiable evidence that the new tools are improving or enhancing the acquisition of skills or accomplishing your desired goal. This is where it is useful to enlist the aid and skill of behavior analysts.
7. *Gather examples of success*. While data are essential, it is critical to have video or living examples that demonstrate clearly how the new tools have improved the task in some way. The scientific data alone are often not enough to convince people to adopt new tools.

8. *Search out and use assessment and feedback.* Even the most successful programs can find areas for improvement. Evaluate the entire teaching process regularly so it can be adjusted and enhanced.

What became so clear to me during our post-symposium discussions was that the steps and strategies for introducing professionals to new tools and ideas are similar across disciplines. I've worked with and seen successful transitions at Guide Dogs for the Blind, various law enforcement agencies, and organizations that have used TAGteach (such as Dr. Levy's surgical teaching program). Again and again, I've seen that being persuasive goes beyond simply understanding the science of learning.

While we know intuitively that using positive reinforcement is helpful and beneficial, convincing others of its power is not always easy, particularly when those needing convincing are teaching professionals who are already skilled and knowledgeable in their specific disciplines. Not surprisingly, doctors who teach surgical skills to medical students are slow to adopt a new teaching method; after all, the techniques they have been using have worked. Sadly, traditional medical teaching methods often include lots of yelling, criticizing, and cajoling (sound familiar?). To persuade other professionals to switch to our methods, we must have more than a well-thought-out and proven process.

There is a factor critical to getting our message to others: we must be careful about how we refer to a new procedure when introducing it to other professionals. If we say our technique is "better," it implies that what our colleagues have been doing is bad or wrong. We must avoid giving that impression, or people will be less open to listening and learning. Instead, we should refer to the procedure as a new tool to add to their toolbox. We can then make a compelling case for the use of that tool but allow them to choose when and if they will use that tool on their own.

The many steps and skills needed to introduce professionals to new skills or ideas can be frustrating, but we should take heart and find hope in the successes we see all around us. This recent breakthrough in the surgical community is just one more great example of the successful use of positive reinforcement and the application of good teaching skills.

Reference

Konkel, Lindsey. "Positive Reinforcement Helps Surgeons Learn." *Scientific American*, 3/9/16. https://www.scientificamerican.com/article/positive-reinforcement-helps-surgeons-learn.

Horses, Butterflies and Surgeons: The Secret to Training Success

During ClickerExpo we often discuss the thrill and the challenges of exposing new people to clicker training and the power of positive reinforcement. One of the biggest challenges when someone in our community tries to introduce positive reinforcement to a new group is that they're often faced with excuses for why it won't or can't work.

I speak to working-dog trainers who face opposition from colleagues who believe that positive reinforcement training either takes too long or is less reliable. We offer a series of seminars on training horses, an area where positive reinforcement is growing. Nevertheless, trainers share with me that frequently they face beliefs that horses are too flighty and will not respond well to positive reinforcement. I've presented the challenges I faced in trying to train 10,000 butterflies to fly on cue in the face of the assertion by many that butterflies are not smart enough to be trained. Theresa McKeon and Karen Pryor faced the opposite obstacle in introducing surgeons to the concept of using positive reinforcement to improve their surgical skills. Early discussions with some surgeons raised concerns that surgeons might be *too intelligent* to respond to learning in this way. The excuses and reasons that those opposed to the use of positive reinforcement present are always varied and, sometimes, contradictory.

Those of us who have been successful working with difficult groups are often asked how we convinced individuals or organizations to accept positive reinforcement. One trainer asked me for the "one-minute elevator speech" that can convince someone to consider the use of positive reinforcement. It was that question that made me realize that perhaps we are too eager to find the easy solution. I began comparing the techniques of those who have been successful teaching positive reinforcement in new arenas, and I discovered that the only thing we had in common was not what you might expect.

Most of us try to persuade others of our point of view by using science, effectiveness, and ethics. These are important parts of the discussion, but they are not enough. We definitely need to have evidence and accurate information if we are to speak intelligently, but the secret to opening the dialogue may surprise you. In each case, the successful trainer was accepting, tolerant, and kind.

Can it really be that simple? To paraphrase Bob Bailey, it's simple but it's not easy. To be effective, tolerance and kindness must be sincere. People will only listen to you if they feel accepted and understood. You can explain the science, you can show the data from effectively run positive reinforcement programs, and you can describe your personal ethics, but you will get nowhere unless you accept that others train differently and you are open and tolerant about those differences.

At ClickerExpo, people asked me how inroads were made in various areas and the answer in almost every case was that *we were invited in.* Susan Friedman holds that trying to convert those who have no interest in hearing our message is a waste of our valuable resources. Sometimes we are so certain that we are right, and we are too eager to prove our point. Instead, we should develop a real rapport with the person first, listen to their full story, and understand their perspective. We must recognize that they have skills that work for them, and that they love their animals as much as we do. Only later will we influence them, but we must wait for them to seek help and ask about our methods. Remember that our positive reinforcement skills work just as effectively with people!

Ultimately, we have to continue to do good work and allow that work to speak for itself. At the same time, we have to be tolerant of other approaches to training. When someone asks how we accomplish a task or inquires about the techniques used, it is important to be kind and approachable if we want anyone to be open to what we have to say. There will always be plenty of ways to help others learn about positive reinforcement.

Acceptance, tolerance, and kindness. Simple? Yes! Overly idealistic? I don't think so! I have seen it work firsthand. In looking for complex answers, sometimes we need to begin in a simple, straightforward place.

Five Keys to Working with Challenging Clients

I often consult with organizations that do not use positive reinforcement primarily. While I find success in that arena, I've encountered other consultants who are unable to work with challenging clients. These consultants are ill-equipped to handle the negotiations, and they lack the communication and human-behavior-science skills required to navigate difficult consults. Here are five tips for being more successful:

1. Keep an open mind.

Approach each new consult with an open mind. Don't make assumptions about what trainers know, how they feel, or how they work. Remember that the trainers in the organizations for which you are consulting have been successful with their current approach. Ask questions and assume that everything is done for a good reason. Be prepared to see things that are new or different and to encounter procedures that you don't understand. Instead of thinking you need to change everything that is different, work hard to understand the needs and goals of the organization. When you are called in for a consult, your clients will tell you what they want your help with; focus on the issues they bring up when you offer advice.

2. Use small approximations.

Just as you do training animals, use small, achievable approximations with your clients. If you see things that you feel need to change or be adjusted, set clear and realistic goals. Don't expect your client to embrace everything you present all at once. As the client makes progress, be ready to reinforce that progress. Too often, we expect clients to drop every old strategy and employ new techniques immediately. That is an unrealistic approach, one that doesn't set them up for success.

3. Learn from clients and create a true partnership.

The individuals who hire us are professionals in their own fields; they possess skills and unique knowledge. Appreciate what they can teach you. If clients see that you understand their perspectives and are invested in their success, they will view you as a valuable partner. My acceptance into the search-and-rescue community, the guide-dog world, and law enforcement agencies only occurred after I had invested a great deal of time working side by side with these groups and making an effort to understand how and why they work the way they do.

4. Keep data and track progress.

Most organizations are willing to accept new strategies if they can see a direct improvement in their success rates. Find the right metrics and show data to assess and quantify progress. In explosive detection, reduction in missed finds and reduction in false alerts were the metrics that mattered most. In narcotic detection, showing that new training techniques help more drug searches hold up in court was the data that made the difference. In the guide-dog community, a reduction in training time, improved accuracy, and improved working temperament was enough to get many organizations to make changes. Facts are your most persuasive tool; the presentation of reliable data can be the strongest motivator for your client.

5. Develop people skills.

I encourage every consultant to spend time learning how to use positive reinforcement with people. So often, trainers who are proficient at using positive reinforcement with animals are unable to deliver reinforcement with people—especially if it involves verbal communication. Stronger people skills also improve negotiation skills, aid in setting priorities with clients, garner better team support and buy-in, and further effective communication.

They have to want to change

We cannot force an organization or an individual to change their habits and working style. We can influence them through actions, compelling data, proven techniques, and through our own good work, but they must discover the need to change on their own. It is important to move clients forward at a pace with which they are comfortable. Influencing them using the techniques described above, we can make significant progress over time.

I know the frustration of trying to convince a colleague to try a new training technique. I have been through the process many times—and have not always had success. In cases where I did achieve success, however, the time and effort were well worth it. I encourage you to consider some of the tips I have described above the next time you work with a challenging client. I promise they will be helpful!

10 Unique and Random Things I Learned During My International Travels

In 2015, I completed a 31-day international trip that included stops in Mexico, France, Spain, the Czech Republic, and multiple stops in the United Kingdom. This trip was a mix of seminars and private consultations where I met many wonderful people and had many great experiences. But I also learned some random, and probably irrelevant, information that I found interesting and worth sharing.

It takes longer in Czech

Whenever I speak somewhere that requires a translator, the organizers arrange for consecutive translation—meaning I say a sentence, then the translator says the sentence. As a result, I expect to cover approximately half the material I would normally cover in the same amount of time if the seminar were in English. Once the translator and I get into a rhythm, frequently we can cover even more material. In Prague, much to my surprise, a standard three-hour seminar required nine hours! A contributing factor may have been that the translator, who was scheduled and who had practiced by watching videos of my lectures, became ill. Her last-minute replacement, who spoke excellent English, was unable to keep up with the unique terms of our profession.

At the first break, one of the attendees offered to help translate. He was excellent, and he had two other translators sitting with him for support. Once in a while during that seminar, when I'd use a term like "behavioral momentum" or "default position," the translator would say, "Please wait!" Then, he and the two translators assisting him would huddle for a lengthy discussion to determine how best to translate that particular phrase.

That evening I worked hard at editing my presentations, simplifying terms where appropriate, and cutting illustrative stories that I knew would not translate well. Day Two went much more smoothly; we even made up for lost time. The Czech hosts have already invited me to return, so next time I will know how to prepare properly!

This was a really good experience; translation is never easy, and my hosts handled it well. There are countless stories I could tell about translation nightmares, but it is helpful to be reminded of the benefit of distilling my messages into their simplest forms—a valuable lesson and reminder for any teacher.

Don't ask "How are you?" unless you really want to know!

In the United States we often greet people with a "How are you?" This greeting is usually meant as an alternative to "Hi" or "Good morning." In the Czech Republic they take the question literally. Each time I, mistakenly, asked, "How are you?" I would receive a long and detailed response. One of my hosts finally explained to me that "How are you?" is not used as a greeting in the Czech language; thus, people responded with a sincere and often personal answer. It only took three times for me to ask the question before I adapted my daily greeting. (I am *not* a one-trial learner.)

Behavioral lessons in politics

I am not a big political follower and certainly do not push my political convictions on others, but I could not help but marvel at some of the political systems I witnessed at work in Europe. England and Spain were both in the middle of elections while I was visiting. The British system limits candidates to a very short campaign period (short at least by US standards). They also restrict the candidates to a limited campaign budget. Boy, would those two things change politics as we know it in the United States! In Spain, I was amazed to see the high turnout for the elections. Perhaps that's because Spaniards hold elections on a Sunday to make it easier for everyone to vote? From training we know that to see behavior change, make it easier for the learner to accomplish the desired task. I see the laws of learning at work everywhere I look.

Nothing wrong with a George Costanza wallet

When I take my wallet out of my pocket, friends and colleagues often make comments about my "George Costanza wallet" because I keep so much stuff in it. Frequently the question is, "Doesn't it throw your back out?" Apparently, there was a *Seinfeld* episode in which the show focused on the character George's very fat wallet.

I carry what I need in my wallet and have never let the comments bother me. During my trip, I was wandering through Leicester Square in Central London in an area that was very heavily populated. (Dwayne Johnson was there for the debut of his film *San Andreas*—people were packed in everywhere). Suddenly I felt someone pushing against my backside, so I quickly spun around, and found a man's hand stuck in my back pocket. He started screaming; I had turned around so quickly that his hand got trapped in my back pocket! Next thing I knew, a police constable was at my side assisting in extricating the pickpocket's hand from my pocket and then arresting the man. The pickpocket was writhing in pain and kept saying that I had broken his wrist, when all I had done was spin around quickly. The constable replied, "You should have kept your hands to yourself." As I helped an additional officer fill out some paperwork, he commented, "That George Costanza wallet kept your valuables safe!" I am now even more pleased with my fat wallet!

Always set a back-up alarm!

I have never been late, or overslept, for a lecture, seminar, or consulting job. In fact, oversleeping is something I have rarely done. But during my travels the first stop after arriving in Europe was Paris, where I was speaking along with Susan Friedman, Kathy Sdao, Grisha Stewart, Joey Iverson, Chirag Patel, Kelly Gorman Dunbar, and Jo-Rosie Haffenden at a four-day dog event. On the second evening, many of us who were still dealing with jet lag decided to go to the Moulin Rouge—the 11:00 pm show!

It had been a long day for me; I did not sleep well the night before, I spoke for the full day, and then I had a late dinner and attended the show with the group. It was after 2:00 am when I finally got to bed. Not that late for me, but given the time difference and the long day, I must have been more tired than I thought, because I fell into a deep sleep. Kathy was speaking the next day and she was set to go to the venue early. The rest of us were going to meet at 8:00 am in the hotel lobby and go over together (it was a bit of a walk combined with a subway ride), and I was one of the group that knew my way there. I don't really know what happened, whether I slept through my alarm or it didn't go off, but I was jolted awake by the phone in my hotel room. I stumbled out of bed and answered the phone. I heard Dr. Susan Friedman's calm and measured voice: "Hi Ken. Were you still planning to meet us at 8:00 am in the lobby?" I remember replying, "Yes! What time is it?" Just as calmly and patiently, Susan said, "8:15." "*What*? I'll be right down!" I screamed incredulously. I splashed water on my face, brushed my teeth, and dressed; I was in the lobby in about eight minutes. The entire team was waiting for me. The only thing worse than oversleeping is having a dozen people waiting for you and having Dr. Susan Friedman be the one to have to wake you up!

I want Grisha Stewart to be my friend

The Paris dog event was a great experience. It is always nice to share the podium with colleagues that I consider to be friends and to meet new colleagues. During Kathy's first day, her computer was causing her some difficulty. She was new to Macs, and her videos just were not playing. Chirag, Susan, and Grisha—all fellow Mac users—were immensely helpful and worked with Kathy all day to resolve the problem. By Day Two, everything worked perfectly for Kathy!

What caught my attention was just how attentive Grisha was to Kathy's needs. The minute there was even a hint of an issue, Grisha would jump up and be poised to help. If Kathy had trouble finding a file, Grisha had learned Kathy's filing structure and was able to quickly and without hesitation tell her what to click on and then guide Kathy to the correct folder. At one point near the end of the day, Kathy was looking at her computer and seemed a bit perplexed. Grisha was out of her seat ready to assist. Turns out Kathy had solved her problem, so Grisha sat down. I remember leaning over to Susan Friedman and whispering, "I wish when I traveled I had a friend like Grisha Stewart to help me!" It was a team effort, but Grisha really shined—selfless and helpful throughout!

Butterflies *are* animals!

One of this trip's highlights was the Butterfly Project (see "The Butterfly Project," p. 123, for details). Because I tweeted about the project frequently and wrote an article about it on the KPCT website, many people asked me questions about it. The one question that I heard several times and that was most surprising was a variation of: "I thought you were an animal trainer; what drew you to training butterflies?" I always responded, "Butterflies are animals!"

One individual thought about my answer a moment, then said, "No, I think they are insects!" I stared, a bit puzzled, wondering why we were not on the same wavelength. Finally, I said, "Yes, they are insects, and insects are animals!"

Ultimately, I was unable to convince this individual, and we agreed to disagree. But I was truly flabbergasted when I had a similar conversation with several other people. I know it is difficult to convince people that training applies to all animals, but I never thought I would have to argue about or convince people about the definition of an animal!

Anything is possible

The previous discussion notwithstanding, the butterfly project reaffirmed my long-held belief that anything is possible if you put your mind to it. A seemingly impossible task: train 10,000 butterflies to fly on cue and do all the training in less than three weeks! I always tell people that if you keep an open mind, do your research, and apply learning principles properly, you can accomplish pretty amazing things, but I must admit this project worried me: Would we fail to accomplish this task? Would we do it in the timeframe we had? I worried that I had bitten off more than I could chew. But the team pulled through and renewed my faith in the power of applying the principles of learning.

I'm a Pepper: the power of a reinforcer

One thing that gives me great pleasure during a seminar is being able to sip an ice-cold Diet Dr. Pepper throughout the seminar. It is a guilty pleasure that I truly enjoy. During this trip to Europe I went almost the entire month without a Diet Dr. Pepper—the drink exists in some places, but it is much harder to find. I concluded my series of seminars with two in the UK, organized by Lynda Taylor of Positive Animal Solutions. She knew of my preference and went out of her way to get a large supply of my favorite beverage. Lynda even had each venue provide a bucket of ice so that I could have the soda ice-cold every day! I was in heaven, and I found myself enjoying the last two seminars more than ever—it was very reinforcing. Each day I found myself thinking about and waiting for my Diet Dr. Pepper. I truly realized the power of a reinforcer that has been unavailable for a long time—it was huge!

No matter how much I know about reinforcers intellectually, I continue to marvel when I see them work on me!

31 days is too long!

I love to travel. I enjoy consulting, and I truly get pleasure from teaching seminars. The people that I meet are wonderful and the experiences are so worthwhile. But I also learned that being away from home for 31 days is too long. In the future, I will make shorter trips, because there is no place like home!

Unexpected Learning

In this chapter I share moments from unforeseen sources that changed my training. These are my personal stories of growth and development that so significantly transformed some aspect of my training that I have never forgotten them. I hope that you can take something away from my experiences that will be useful to you.

What's in a Handshake?

Dolphin trainers often teach their animals to rise out of the water to target or touch the animal's pectoral fin to the trainer's hand. Trainers refer to this behavior as a "pec shake" or "pec touch" behavior. It appears to the public as if the dolphin is shaking hands with the trainer. Trainers frequently use this behavior in shows in the form of a greeting, and it is a fun way to introduce the animal to the audience.

As a young trainer, I had seen many dolphins exhibit this behavior, and I had trained it myself with several dolphins. The criteria were clear; the animal was to touch my hand as he reached the height of his vertical ascent. The moment the dolphin's pec fin touched my hand, I blew my whistle, my marker, then followed that with a favorite fish as a reinforcer. I observed trainers at other facilities demonstrate this behavior with their dolphins and they always appeared to have the exact same criteria.

After about five years as a trainer, I reached a point where I was feeling confident in my knowledge and skills. I visited a dolphin facility and watched one of their shows. The trainer was narrating the show while training two bottlenose dolphins. At the start of the show she introduced her two dolphins to the audience while reaching out to touch each animal's pec fin. The behavior was identical to the behavior I had trained and seen performed thousands of times. The only difference was that this trainer blew her whistle late! Instead of blowing the whistle when the animal touched her hand, she blew the whistle after the animal re-entered the water. I remember thinking, "Rookie trainer! She's going to mess up that behavior." I saw a second show later that day, and she did the exact same thing. "Oh well," I thought, "not every trainer is as careful or as precise as they should be."

Several years later, I was visiting a friend and colleague, Lisa, who worked for the same company as the trainer I had seen make that training mistake years earlier. During a dolphin show I saw Lisa make the same mistake! She blew the whistle as the dolphin re-entered the water. Because I knew Lisa well, I felt comfortable asking why she marked the behavior when she did. I expected her to be embarrassed that she had made such an obvious error. Instead, she explained, "In our company we always narrate as we train. We don't want the dolphin to soak our microphone with salt water, so we blow our whistle if the animal re-enters the water cleanly without making a splash."

Well, that made perfect sense! Didn't I feel like a fool? I had jumped to the conclusion that the young trainer I watched years earlier had made a mistake. But she had handled the situation perfectly—I was the one who had made an error. I made an assumption about what criterion she should be looking for. The reality is that most behaviors have multiple different criteria, and the most important criteria will vary depending on the animal, the trainer, the facility, and the circumstances.

I will never forget the impact of this lesson. We get so comfortable in our own world and experiences that we forget that there may be alternative ways to accomplish the same task. We must be careful not to jump to conclusions when we watch others train; it is far too easy to criticize and assume the worst. Today, when I observe a trainer make a decision that perplexes me, I assume the best. There may be a goal I don't understand or perhaps a tool is being used that is unfamiliar to me. On occasion, I still make snap judgements about something I see, but then I recall my experience with the simple "handshake" behavior and I pause—and reconsider. Even if my initial perception proves to be true, taking the time to ask a few questions and give my response more thought sets up a more constructive and positive interaction.

No Love for the Holidays?

A while ago, as summer ended and we were moving toward fall, I was contacted by a large marketing firm that was making a Chicago-area Public Service Announcement (PSA) encouraging people to consider adopting their next pet from a shelter. It was going to be a big-budget, well-produced commercial, funded by a generous benefactor. I have been a strong supporter of many Chicago-area shelters, and I am a big proponent of pet adoptions everywhere I speak and teach. I was honored to have the opportunity to be a spokesperson and trainer of several dogs for this high-profile television spot.

A veteran of film

I looked forward to my first meeting with the production team, to discuss my role in the commercial and to acquire a better understanding of the behaviors they needed trained. I am not new to the world of television and film production. I am aware that even a simple film-shoot can be filled with complications and prove to be challenging! The dogs have to be well-trained; desensitized to lots of people, lots of strange-looking equipment, rapid movement of booms and trolleys, bright lights, and cables; and able to work for long periods of time with an unpredictable number of repetitions. (The behavior needs to look as good the 25th time as it did the 1st time it was performed.)

Usually the biggest challenge is the inevitable reality of the director changing his or her mind about what the dog should do—halfway through the shoot! The trainer and the dog must be adaptable, flexible, and ready for just about anything.

To be successful at this type of work, a trainer has to be more than just skilled at training; working on a set requires being a good negotiator. You have to put the animal's needs first, deciding what is best for the animal's health, training, and comfort. But you also have to be open to the many changes and types of direction that the production crew throws at you. Trainers who are inflexible about what the animal can do and who are unwilling to accommodate any requested changes will be labeled as uncooperative very quickly—and will likely not get any future jobs training on a film or video production. You must strike a delicate balance; protecting animal needs and comfort is a priority, but being able to work with the production crew and find solutions that will help the crew members get what they need is also important.

The animal part of this commercial spot looked as though it were going to be easy—simple shots of a variety of dogs playing with a number of different children in assorted locations. Before my first production meeting I had not received a script, so I had no idea what lines I needed to say. I only had a full list of shots: which dogs doing what activities under what conditions. A few simple, but key, behaviors were going to have to be trained, but most of the shots would really be simple, natural play—getting the best shots from actual unscripted play interactions between dogs and kids. This approach does not guarantee any particular shot, but, when you are working with dogs and children, it often comes off more naturally. You can get some really wonderful, and sometimes unexpected, gems. So I went into the meeting ready with questions and suggestions for how we could maximize opportunities to keep dogs and kids safe and get the best shots. I thought I was well prepared for that meeting; I had no idea how wrong I was!

A perfect start

The meeting started out great! We were doing a PSA for a good cause that all of us believed in. We had a good budget, a good director, a good production team, and access to some wonderful dogs. During the first two hours, our meeting flowed well; we all went into the first short break excited about this project. One of the writers from the marketing firm, who had designed and written the commercial, introduced himself and handed me an actual script. He explained that I had been given the key tag line and appeal to the audience at the very end of the commercial. Great! I was looking forward to reading the script. But the break ended, so I did not have the chance to review the actual script until lunch, a few hours later.

"Support your local shelter" was the name of this project, and I knew I was on board with that. The script was simple, straightforward, and very sentimental—it had the earmarks of an effective and emotional ad that would certainly bring people into Chicago-area shelters (they were planning to shoot so that the PSA could be used nationally if it was successful).

After some wonderfully cute shots of dogs, puppies, cats, and kittens playing with kids in adorable settings, all with appropriate adult supervision and attention to good safety practices and set to emotional holiday-themed music, there would be a shot of me teaching two kids how to train their dog.

I was even allowed to use a clicker! As I read the script, I remember thinking, "This is going to be great!"

Good intentions gone wrong

Then, I turned the page to read the last scene, with the final spoken message: I would look into the camera and say, "Give a little love for the holidays! Visit your local shelter and give a deserving pet a home!" A touching scene of a little girl hugging a cute puppy would follow. Powerful stuff, created by a famous and effective marketing team.

Well, it had never occurred to me that I might have an issue with the script; that was not even in the realm of possibilities as far as I was concerned. I was focused on the animal part of the commercial, which is where I expected to have challenges. You see, I have strong reservations about promoting pets as gifts. January is one of the months when shelters receive the most animals. When someone in a home receives a dog or a cat as a Christmas present, many times the family is simply not prepared for all that is involved in adopting the animal and being a pet parent.

The commercial spot was almost too good! I feared it would be much too effective at getting people to choose a pet as a gift; gift-givers would not consider fully the careful thought and preparation needed. Far too often pet gifts are surprises that the recipient has not had the time to consider or prepare for. Pet parents need to be well-informed, ready for the care and training required for a good safe home.

I was concerned that the commercial sent the wrong message, and would ultimately be responsible for the wrong result. My prediction was that Chicago-area shelters would see a huge increase in adoptions during the month of December because of this PSA, and then set new records for dogs and cats returned to the shelter in January!

I wondered who had approved this commercial? Had a specific shelter paid for it or advised on content? I needed to find out. I was going to have to pull out my best negotiating skills to navigate through the landmine that the production team, especially the team that created the commercial, didn't even know they were facing. On that production meeting day, I felt compelled to make my case when we returned from lunch.

Explosive reaction and a new name: Scrooge

The fireworks I set off in that fancy conference room that afternoon in downtown Chicago could be felt and heard for miles! The creative team members who designed the commercial were furious with me. It was very late in the process to make changes, but I had not received a script until that morning, and the PSA was never referred to as a holiday spot, just a "support your local shelter" spot. (It turns out that no shelter or adoption organization had approved the message; the PSA was being paid for by a wealthy benefactor who wanted to do a good thing.) I offered alternative positive messages about pet care and training for the holidays, but those did not go over very well.

Next, I proposed a number of compromises, and encouraged the creative team to bring in a few leaders from Chicago shelters and solicit their opinions. If the shelter folks disagreed with me, then I would step aside and let them proceed; I wouldn't be the spokesperson. But because the local shelters were not the clients, the creative team refused to "waste their time" doing that. I suggested that I speak with their client, the benefactor, and help him understand what was wrong with the PSA concept. But by then I was already perceived as a troublemaker; no one wanted me to go near the man who had given them so much money for this project.

After being called a Scrooge and accused of being someone that "did not believe in love for the holidays," I was placed on the naughty list by that particular ad agency. I had ruined what they were certain would be a CLIO-award-winning ad (the CLIO is an international award given to commercials and other forms of advertising).

Postmortem

I doubted myself for a few days and wondered if I was being too strongly opinionated, which is not normal for me. I always have opinions but am not usually the first to voice them. But when I consulted with several of my contacts at local shelters, they agreed with me that the direct, holiday-themed appeal was probably not the best way to get the "visit your local shelter" message out there.

Fortunately, the funding for the PSA was not lost. After several weeks of negotiating, finally it was decided to re-script the appeal for later. I probably won't be part of that project, but that is fine. At least a better message will be out there. As much as I want to see every animal in a shelter find a forever home, I want to make sure that finding homes for shelter dogs is done with thought and care. We shouldn't be satisfied with any message—it needs to be the right message.

Tulip Joins The Ranch

As 2017 came to a close, I acquired a two-year-old female Maremma sheepdog named Tulip. The Maremma is a livestock-guarding dog, often referred to as an LGD. These dogs were first brought to the United States in the 1970s; they have been used as LGD in the mountains of central Italy for hundreds of years. As there are coyotes in the forest surrounding The Ranch, I felt that a guardian dog would be the best way to deter predators.

The dog as teacher

Originally, I had planned to get two puppies, raising and training them myself, but Tulip was available. She needed a new home, and she was already trained. When I teach students new concepts, I prefer using well-trained animals. I find that working with an experienced animal sets up the student for success; otherwise, the student and the animal are both trying to learn at the same time, and neither is set up for the best learning experience. Since I was new to livestock-guarding dogs and had a lot to learn, I realized that starting out with an experienced dog would be a good first step for me. Tulip could help protect the animals at The Ranch and be my teacher at the same time. I have already learned so much in the few weeks I have worked with Tulip.

Finding wisdom in experience

When my dog's breeder taught me how to handle and train Tulip, her descriptions and stories were far from scientific. She said things like, "The Maremma is a proud dog and an independent thinker," or "The dog must feel as if the herd he is guarding is his, not yours, if you want him to be successful." The breeder reminded me of my Uncle Sam who used similar descriptions to explain how he worked with his herding dogs on his ranch in New Mexico. As a trainer who tries to avoid labels, I listen to the ranchers'/ breeders' wisdom and "translate" it to myself in ways that align with my understanding of animal behavior.

"They must feel that they are in charge"

Two statements I hear and read often are that the Maremma dogs must "feel that they are in charge and that the herd is theirs," and that I must "allow them to make their own decisions as often as possible; they are independent thinkers." I believe these statements point to the fact that much of the work that these dogs do is instinctive; they are reacting to the environment and behaving in ways that come naturally to them. Their cues and their reinforcers come from the environment around them—not from the handlers. If we are not careful, we can interfere with the innate behaviors of these dogs.

Livestock-guarding dogs are territorial, and they are protective of what they believe is theirs. The "resource-guarding" that we find so unacceptable in most dogs is exactly what we desire in a guardian dog. LGD are reinforced by seeing outsiders and predators leave when they bark. Ranchers who are instructed to let the dogs "feel that they are in charge" are less likely to discipline nuisance behaviors and lower the dogs' confidence. A confident dog bred for territorial aggression will claim more territory than an insecure dog. Ranchers who are instructed to let the dogs "feel that the herd is theirs" will have the dogs sleep with the herd, establishing the dogs' territory.

The belief that these dogs should be allowed to "make their own decisions" also highlights the fact that control is a powerful reinforcer for all animals (and humans). When an animal has the freedom to control its environment, and, most importantly, control outcomes (reinforcers and punishers), you have a highly motivated, confident learner, and one that is more likely to stand up to an intruder.

Don't teach them to sit, lie down, or come—*ever!*

Another piece of advice about Maremmas that seemed odd to me at first was, "They cannot be taught basic obedience skills like sit, down, and heel—ever." LGD handlers feel strongly that training basic obedience will ruin the dog as a livestock-guarding dog.

This idea seemed hard for me to believe at first, and I am not sure exactly what behavioral truths are behind it. But after watching these dogs work, I think that perhaps this idea ties in to how critical it is that the dogs be focused on the environment. Cues for what to do are coming from the field, the forest, the street, and the herd—not from the trainer. Perhaps a herding dog that is too interested in people as a source of reinforcement will focus less on its environment, or sleep less during the day and be tired at night when the guarding work is required. Perhaps training will make the dog too friendly to strangers, or, if the training is aversive, cause the dog to be less confident and less territorial. I wonder.

I plan to teach Tulip a recall and a few other behaviors as they become necessary, but I am in no rush to do so. I will be careful about the context in which I train new behaviors that are not related to her role as a livestock-guarding dog. I feel certain that I can do this, but I also recognize that I have a great deal to learn. I will not be cavalier about going against the instructions from the experienced LGD handlers who have been so generous with their advice. After all, ranchers, farmers, and shepherds have been working with guardian dogs for centuries. Although they are not usually schooled in the science of training, they have developed techniques that have proven successful in teaching Maremmas.

What if they misbehave?

Despite asserting that the dogs must make their own decisions and humans should not interfere, LGD trainers emphasize the importance of not allowing the dogs to learn bad habits. Bad habits might include chasing the livestock they are supposed to protect or not allowing you or other people who work with the livestock to come into the pasture. I was told, "If they misbehave, reprimand them immediately, then praise them when they comply because they can be very sensitive." At first, I was a bit alarmed by these instructions until I watched the way one of the trainers handled that very situation. One of the dogs began chasing a donkey, so the trainer called the dog's name and stepped in between the dog and the donkey. The dog veered off and returned to the trainer, and the trainer immediately began praising and petting the dog. In essence, the trainer redirected her to a more appropriate behavior and then reinforced that desirable response. I have used this redirection technique most of my career, but I would never have recognized it from the original description.

A learning partnership

My time with Tulip has just begun and my perspectives and thoughts about her training will certainly evolve. I will have new opportunities to explore how far I can take my partnership with a wonderful animal like Tulip. I am sure that Tulip will be teaching me far more than I will be teaching her.

The Apache Horse "Trainers"

I recently visited my family in southern New Mexico. While I was there, I was introduced to a family friend, a Native American from the Mescalero Apache tribe, whom I will refer to as Tommy. The Mescalero Apache were a nomadic tribe that kept little in the way of physical belongings, and they preserved their cultural history through storytelling. Tommy is one of those storytellers, and over the course of two days he shared many stories with me.

The stories that intrigued me most were the ones about how skilled Apache warriors developed partnerships with their horses. As I listened, I began to hear training strategies that were familiar to me, even though Tommy never used the words "teaching," or "training."

I was reminded of what Susan Friedman always says: "Behavior is a natural science." People who work with animals often come up with similar solutions to problems, even if they are not exposed to the science, because the laws of learning are always at play. Skilled observers of behavior see and use what works and avoid what does not. I hope you will recognize the science hidden within the stories Tommy told me.

Rather than bog down Tommy's stories with my interpretations, I have chosen to share the stories the way he told them and provide numerical references that you can read later with my thoughts about each story.

Tommy's stories, as he told them:

We have not always been horse people. The Apaches had never seen horses before the 1500s, when they were introduced into our mountains by the Spaniards. When we first saw horses, we thought they were odd creatures and we called them Big Dogs. We recognized the advantages of riding horses, though, and our warriors became expert horsemen, much better than the Spaniards or the White men that followed. After horses were welcomed into our tribe, they became essential to the warrior's way of life.

There were many skills required to become a full Mescalero Apache warrior: accuracy with a weapon, stealth, knowledge of the land, tracking skills, and a partnership with a horse.

A warrior's horse was a true partner. After a battle or scouting mission, the horse was cared for, fed, and watered before the warrior had his own dinner. Immediately after riding, the horse would approach the warrior and lift each foot one at a time for the warrior to apply a healing paste to each foot and wrap it in corn husks to keep the feet strong and ready for the next ride. Horses were given immediate access to a grazing pasture and water after each ride, but the horses always chose to ask the warrior for foot care first.[1]

Apache men and their horses prepared for battle together at a young age. Young men learned to ride before they were 12 years old, and used the tools introduced by the Spaniards: saddles, bits, multiple bridles, and spurs. But these tools were considered necessary only until a bond and relationship had been established with the horse. For a true warrior, these tools were not needed. Warriors rode bareback, so the team could communicate more effectively, creating balance and a spiritual connection. The only tools a warrior needed were a rope to guide his horse, and a weapon. The Spanish and the White man never achieved that level of partnership, as they did not respect their horses. [2]

Not all horses became warrior partners; the horses had to prove that they were brave and would not be fearful in battle. Many Apache enemies used guns, and gunfire would startle young horses. The bow and arrow were preferred weapons for Apache warriors, but our young men were trained in the use of rifles. During rifle practice, young men not participating in practice would be in the field with their horses. As soon as rifle practice began, the young men would hang bags of grain around their horses' necks, allowing each horse to feed.[3] *Horses that remained calm became warrior partners, and they were no longer fed during rifle practice. The best horses would seek out their warrior partner during rifle practice, requesting to go into battle. Because there was no battle, the warrior would appease his horse partner by providing his horse with a bag of grain.*[4] *Warriors took great pride in the fact that their horses wanted to go to battle.*

Closing thoughts

As I listened to Tommy's stories, I appreciated the perspective the Mescalero Apaches had about their relationship with their horses. I was fascinated by the training that was clearly taking place, and the techniques that were used long before they were given names by Thorndike, Watson, Skinner, or Pavlov. When you look at stories like this, you can see the laws of behavior at work. I find this fascinating and enjoy digging deeper into traditional stories to try to understand the science at work. I was pleased that Tommy gave me permission to recount these stories and spent so much time answering my questions. I hope you found them as interesting as I did.

Footnotes and Comments

Listening to Tommy's stories, I always tried to read between the lines. I asked many questions, and the story as I have related it includes the original story along with the answers to my questions.

[1]This appears to be an early example of husbandry training, teaching the horse to cooperate in its own care. Apparently, the horses offered the foot voluntarily for the reinforcement of the soothing feel and comfort provided. I asked whether the warrior prodded or pulled at the foot to get the horse to lift it, but Tommy insisted that it was always the horse's choice to lift the foot on its own. In fact, it was considered one of many signs that a true partnership was developing.

[2]There are many ways to interpret this part of the story. I chose to look at the goal of avoiding saddles, spurs, and bits to be an example of truly caring for the horse and trying to put its welfare first. I suppose it could be seen as a macho ritual that had nothing to do with respect, but my feeling and sense from Tommy was that the warrior truly cared about his horse and had great respect for the horse and their partnership.

[3]This sounds a lot like a counter-conditioning procedure! I asked Tommy many times over our two days of discussions if the food was given before or after the rifles were being fired, and he always answered definitively, "After." I also asked if the warriors would wait until the rifles had been fired for several minutes, and Tommy said, "No, it was always immediately after the rifle practice began."

[4]The "request to go to battle" is an interesting way to describe what is taking place, but it is a great example of the stories that we often develop to explain behavior. I think these were experienced horses that had learned that the sound of rifles meant food, and they learned to seek their warrior out when the grain was not offered immediately.

From Russia with Love

In 2014, I spent two weeks consulting in Russia, conducting a series of seminars for trainers from at least 10 different zoos and aquariums. It was an interesting experience as my translator stood next to me for the full seminar—I would say a sentence, then he would translate that sentence, and that continued all day every day for each seminar. I was surprised at how quickly we got into a rhythm and the seminars began to flow well. The Russian trainers were an eager audience, and I was amazed to find that I had an odd celebrity status over there.

A book with no boundaries

Much to my surprise, my book *Animal Training: Successful Animal Management through Positive Reinforcement* was everywhere—in Russian! There were probably more copies of my book in Russia than in any country I have ever visited, possibly because it is available there through two different publishers. Interestingly, these two Russian editions are not sanctioned versions of the book; my US publisher and I had no idea there were two Russian editions in circulation. I have been working for many years with translators in France, Japan, and Mexico, and it has been a massively difficult undertaking, so I was surprised to find my book had already been translated into Russian, twice! Just the fact that it is available so widely in Russia was amazing to me. There was the St. Petersburg edition, which is a handsomely bound leather version of the book that is even larger than the English version; the Moscow edition is divided into three large paperback volumes. Every professional trainer in Russia seems to have the book (and I am not using hyperbole). It is crazy how many people have one of the two Russian editions. The Russian trainers claimed that I am one of the most famous trainers in Russia! Who knew?

The same challenge world-over

It was interesting for me to see that trainers are the same all over the world. I met and watched some of the best exotic animal trainers I have ever seen. Yet, despite their skill and accomplishment, their most common question was, "How do I train my dog?" We all tend to be very species- (or breed-) focused and often have difficulty understanding how to translate our knowledge to a different type of animal.

Grasping the power of relationships

Perhaps one of the most difficult things for me during this consulting trip was trying to meet the Russians' desire for a serious critique of their training. They had me watch a training session or show, then the entire staff gathered together as the supervisor asked, "Tell us, what did we do wrong?" I made a few suggestions and often found myself wanting to compliment them on some amazing behavior they had trained. Invariably their response to the compliment was a dismissive, "Well, I learned it from your book" or "I just followed the instructions in your book." Sometimes I was so blown away by a specific behavior that I had to ask, "Show me where in my book you learned *that*!"

On the whole, the Russians proved to be a skilled and disciplined group—which goes a long way in making much of their training so clean and precise. I think what was new to them, or that they didn't quite understand, was the power and importance of relationships in training. They recognized that relationships existed, but that fact was just not logical enough for them to embrace relationships completely as a useful tool at first. During each seminar I spent an entire day focused on non-food reinforcers and demonstrated how relationships fit into making those reinforcers more successful—a topic I have been teaching at ClickerExpo for many years. Most of my Russian colleagues had adopted positive reinforcement but were focused entirely on food. By teaching them how to develop novel reinforcers such as clapping, petting, and game play, they were able to expand their available menu of reinforcement options. Not only did this make it easier for them to apply reinforcers in situations where food was not easy to use, but it improved the relationship with their animals, which allowed them to train more difficult and complex behaviors because they had developed a high level of trust. It was great to see the light bulb go on in their heads, since some of these concepts were the newest and most transformative for them.

Russian reinforcement for Ken

The Russian language is new to me, but when I travel anywhere, I try to learn a few basic words. I went to the first seminar in my first city and started by saying good morning in Russian. Up until that point the attendees had been quiet and reserved, but, after just two Russian words out of my mouth, they all came to life, applauded, and cheered. So on day two, I learned a new phrase and in Russian I said, "Good morning! Welcome back!" The trainers were even more appreciative than the first day. Finally, on the third day, I practiced for several hours and started the seminar by saying in Russian, "Good morning! Today I will present the seminar entirely in Russian." I got a standing ovation and even when I admitted that I really couldn't do that, and I didn't think they would want me to try, they laughed and applauded their approval yet again. It wasn't until later that I realized how powerful that small positive reinforcement experience had been. They weren't collectively trying to get me to speak more Russian; they were just genuinely pleased that I tried. But I was so thrilled by their reaction that I was really motivated to keep learning more! Despite the fact that I know positive reinforcement is powerful, I still marvel when I see it occur so naturally and work so well!

Horse husbandry, and more autographs

Something that I wasn't planning was a trip to the Kazan Hippodrome—a fabled and magnificent horse racing track, equestrian center, and museum in the heart of the Republic of Tatarstan. My hosts insisted that I go and that the trainers there would love to meet me. I explained that horse trainers don't really follow my style of training in most cases, and certainly not at a horse track. But they persisted and took me anyway.

I was so glad that I went! The track was the most modern and advanced animal facility I had seen so far in Russia. Hundreds of horses were housed there in the most modern, heated, and spacious stables I had ever experienced. There was a state-of-the-art hospital and, compared to everything else I had seen related to animal care in Russia, this was the height of luxury.

No fewer than a dozen Russian horse trainers greeted me eagerly and showed me around their facility. They pulled out copies of my book for me to sign—and I felt compelled to ask if they actually used this book to guide them in training horses. They vigorously nodded their heads "yes" and I asked, "Really? To train them for equestrian events and horse racing?" They laughed and said emphatically, "*No!*" I inquired, "Well, then, how do you use my book?" One of them opened my book to the chapter on husbandry training and smiled while giving me a big thumbs-up! They then led me to the hospital where they introduced me to several Orlov horses (a Russian breed). The trainers demonstrated how the horses were trained with positive reinforcement for positioning for X-rays, for foot care, for baths, and grooming—all using a whistle and treats. I commented on how wonderful what they were showing me was, and their response (just like the zoo trainers I had met) was, "Well, we learned it from you!" I was speechless and my eyes welled up with tears. They became very concerned that they had done something wrong. My translator stepped in and explained that they were good tears, "like when you eat good Russian mustard!"

Onward to spread the positive message

I could tell all sorts of stories about Russian food (like the very spicy Russian mustard), travel adventures on Russian airlines, or the awful experience I had trying to drink fermented horse's milk, but I will save those stories for another time. Each time I travel to a new place, it renews my conviction that spreading the word about positive reinforcement training is vital and that helping people learn to train better is a worthwhile and important endeavor. There will always be new people to teach and new things to learn—that's what keeps me traveling. I learned a great deal during my trip and can't thank the trainers and my hosts enough for their wonderful hospitality. I am not sure if it was life imitating art, but I was tickled that they signed their cards and notes with the words, "From Russia with Love."

The Unexpected Benefits of Training

We discuss the benefits of training and the advantages of positive reinforcement quite frequently, but I have long believed that training does far more than we realize. Positive reinforcement training expands animals' repertoires, makes them better problem-solvers, increases their resilience to change and, dare I say it, boosts their intelligence. The evidence of these benefits is anecdotal, but I would suggest that the examples below present a compelling case for supporting these claims.

Escape from predation

A friend and colleague of mine, Ilana Bram, shared a story from a local co-op where she trains goats to do various husbandry behaviors. The co-op also has chickens living on site, and Ilana began training one hen in particular named Chickie. Chickie really took to the training and was an eager learner, developing a small but solid repertoire of behaviors.

Sadly, a few weeks ago raccoons got into the enclosure and killed almost all of the chicken population. Only four birds survived the attack, and Chickie was one of them. Ilana asked if I thought Chickie's exposure to training contributed to her ability to escape the attack. She pointed out, quite accurately, that training had expanded Chickie's behavioral repertoire, which included climbing on objects, flying short distances, and being exposed to new areas within the enclosure. Ilana said that Chickie's personality seemed to change after the training; she was more daring and exploratory, venturing farther out than the other chickens and boldly soliciting treats from people. Might these changes have given her a survival advantage?

I immediately responded, "Yes!" I believe that training gives animals new skills and makes them better problem-solvers. We will never know for sure whether those skills made a difference to Chickie on that terrible night, but I believe they did. This incident brought to mind other examples of well-trained animals showing resilience and accomplishing incredible things.

Earthquake survival

I spent several years as the trainer for a group of more than 200 birds in a park in Mexico City. The population included several species of parrots, ravens, toucans, birds of prey, and a variety of songbirds. These birds lived in social groups in large free-flight aviaries. We did basic training with all the birds, but we focused most of our attention and advanced training on the birds that were part of our daily shows. The complexity of training varied from species to species, but included flying on cue, medical behaviors, tactile behaviors, vocalizations, and lots of socialization and desensitization to new people and places.

Early one morning, Mexico City experienced a devastating earthquake that registered 8.0 on the Richter scale and created widespread damage in the area. When I arrived at the park, I found that, although three of the aviaries were still standing, two had sustained serious damage. A large building next to the enclosures had collapsed, and huge slabs of concrete and shards of glass had torn holes in the aviary and crushed or buried sections of the birds' homes.

As we inspected the area, what we found was heartbreaking. Most of the 62 birds who lived in the damaged aviaries had died, primarily from inhaling smoke and dust created by the collapsed building. Words cannot describe the pain we experienced over the wonderfully bright lives that were lost that morning.

But something miraculous also had happened; we discovered 17 birds that had somehow survived and made their way to safety. The birds were hanging out in three different places. They had found their way to the trainer's office, the flight training area, and the show stage. Of the 17 birds that lived, 14 were birds from our show. They included five macaws, three ravens, two Amazon parrots, two cockatoos, and two toucans. Only two birds from our show failed to escape the disaster.

Given the variety of species involved, their escape from two different aviaries, the unusual routes and extraordinary effort to get to where we found them, and the large number of similar species living in the same space that did not survive, it seems more than a coincidence that it was mostly the well-trained birds that found their way to safety. All of the birds had spent time in the training locations and had access to those spaces; the only difference was that they had not had the same complex and extensive training. We could not find any other logical explanation.

Late night fishing

On a lighter note, I would like to share the story of a California sea lion named Jones that I worked with in Texas. We were doing some renovations to one of our sea lion habitats, so we relocated Jones and six other males to a temporary home located right next to a large lake. Jones was an older, well-trained, very experienced animal. The other six seals were rescued animals that we had adopted recently, and, although they were part of our training program, they were still in the early stages of training.

The sea lions had been living in their temporary habitat for about six weeks when we began to notice that Jones was starting his mornings very slowly. He was healthy and bright-eyed, but he behaved as though he had just eaten a huge meal. We knew this wasn't the case because his last meal had been the night before. Sea lions have voracious appetites, and Jones would still eat his morning meal, but he ate slowly and seemed full. The veterinarian found no signs of illness, and we were baffled.

This unusual behavior had gone on for almost two weeks when in the wee hours of the morning I received a phone call from one of our night security officers. He claimed that he saw a large animal in the lake. I knew that the only animals living in the lake were fish, nothing large like our security guard was describing, so I went into the park to investigate.

It was still dark at 4:00 am when I arrived to check out the mysterious report. In the moonlight, I could see a large body break the surface of the water, then quickly disappear below the surface. It took me several minutes to recognize the distinct form of a sea lion! But how was that possible? I dashed over to the sea lion habitats in alarm.

When I arrived at the habitat next to the lake, I noticed immediately that there were six instead of seven animals. Jones was missing. That must be him in the lake! I inspected the habitat carefully. No open doors; they were all locked. No holes, gaps, or openings in the fence or wall. How did he get out? Had he really been fishing in the lake like this for the past two weeks? It didn't make sense.

I decided not to call him over nor alert him to my presence. I found a comfortable spot to sit and observe out of sight. At 5:45 am, as the sun began to rise, Jones made his way out of the lake. He paused in the shallow beach water and seemed to be looking around, as if to make sure nobody was looking (am I being anthropomorphic, or what!). Then he waddled over to his habitat, approached the shortest part of the fence, and stood up on his rear flippers. This is not a natural behavior, but one that I had taught him years before. He was barely able to place his chin on the top of the fence. Then, with a Herculean effort, he used his chin to pull himself up, while using his front and rear flippers to walk up the wall. None of this was typical sea lion behavior. After a 5-minute struggle, he pulled his 550-pound frame to the top of the fence and plopped to the ground on the inside of his habitat. He proceeded to get comfortable in his favorite sleeping spot, exactly where we find him every morning!

The next evening, I watched Jones again from my hiding spot. About an hour after closing, Jones woke up from his slumber, paced the entire exhibit as if looking to make sure nobody was watching (yes, anthropomorphic again). Then he carefully reversed the process, climbing out of the exhibit, just as I had watched him climb back in that morning. It was obviously difficult and required some balancing skill, strength, and determination, but he eventually made it over the fence and went straight for the lake. There he foraged for fish all night long, returning home at sunrise, just as he had done the night before.

I feel certain that Jones' 10-year training experience, regular exercise of his neck and flipper muscles, and his trained repertoire of climbing and standing made his fishing expeditions possible. Was his impeccable timing of climbing in and out when he could not be observed related to his expanded problem-solving ability? Could his desire to come back every morning be a sign that he clearly enjoyed interactions with his trainers? It didn't seem as if he returned just to get a free breakfast; he showed little interest in eating from us when he returned! I believe this story demonstrates a variety of ways that training gives animals a wider repertoire of skills.

So many other examples

These three stories just scratch the surface; I have worked with many animals that demonstrated unique and untrained problem-solving skills. There was a dolphin, Misty, who learned to collect trash and hide it away in a drain like a bank account so that she could cash it in for fish when she felt the need. Ranbir the gibbon, upon seeing a wild snake enter his habitat, figured out how to hide in a restraint box and lock himself in so that he was safely out of harm's way. Service dog Lambo, faced with a fire and an unconscious owner, took the initiative to grab the sleeping baby by the onesie and carry it to the neighbor's house. Lambo's action got the owner help in time and ultimately saved the lives of all involved. We see examples in the service and guide dog worlds all the time of dogs that go far beyond what they were trained to do and accomplish the improbable.

Final thoughts

Training expands animals' views of their world and enables them to accomplish tasks that had not been specifically trained. Positive reinforcement opens up learners' thinking and allows them to explore and grow with greater confidence. Animals trained with punishment tend to have the opposite happen; their worldview shrinks and they are hesitant to try new things. Positive reinforcement training sets up animals to be eager learners and makes it possible for them to accomplish far more than what we train purposefully. The more I am exposed to the power and benefits of positive training, the more impressed I am by the possibilities and the remarkable ways that animals benefit.

The Power of Relationships

During my first few years as a trainer, I worked with a group of young bottlenose dolphins at a marine-life park in Texas. I have fond memories of two young male dolphins from that group, Hastings who was shy but playful and Lucky who was a survivor of a fishing net entanglement in the Gulf of Mexico. I was assigned to Lucky's rehabilitation effort, and Hastings was one of Lucky's first companions. I spent hours each day playing with and training Lucky and Hastings. In many ways, they were my first and best training teachers.

The tail game

Together we developed a fun game that both dolphins enjoyed. I held their tails while tickling and massaging them, which caused them to relax and close their eyes. Their bodies went limp as I held their tails, and they allowed me to push them under water then pull their tails up a few feet above the water's surface. I repeated this over and over until my arms wore out. After 15 minutes, my biceps burned as if I had been lifting weights, but Lucky and Hastings never seemed to tire of the game.

A relationship forms

Other trainers tried to replicate the game, but neither Lucky nor Hastings allowed others to play. Both dolphins enjoyed a good rubdown from the other trainers but never allowed those trainers to play with their tails. Whenever trainers tried the game, Lucky and Hastings swam away, uninterested in playing, or, if I was there, they swam over to me. I remember one of the senior trainers telling me, "That means they trust you. No animal likes to have their means of locomotion restrained; their tails are how they power through the water. They would never let you hold them like that if they didn't completely trust you!" I remember feeling proud that I had gained their trust. I felt as though I had forged a real relationship with Lucky and Hastings.

After working with Lucky and Hastings for three years, I was offered an opportunity to move to Mexico City to work as a trainer with a new, diverse group of animals. The idea of gaining new experiences and working with new animals was exciting, but it also meant saying goodbye to the many animals I had come to know and love for the previous three years. My last day in Texas was sad: I knew I would miss the staff and, most of all, I would miss the animals, especially Lucky and Hastings. The last thing I did on my final day was to play the tail game with my two favorite dolphins. I think we played for 45 minutes. I didn't want the playtime to end, and neither did Lucky nor Hastings. I knew I was leaving them in good hands; they had great relationships with many other trainers, but saying goodbye to them was still hard.

A special reunion

I was in Mexico for just over two-and-a-half years and never had the chance to get back to Texas for a visit. But when my contract in Mexico ended, I was asked to return to Texas, and I was excited to be reunited with my trainer and animal friends. On my first day back, my supervisor was touring me around the area showing me things that were new and reintroducing me to all the animals. There had been lots of changes, but it felt so familiar and comfortable. As we approached the dolphin habitat, my supervisor began pointing out who was who. Most of the animals were very familiar to me, but they had grown, and it had been more than two years since I had seen them.

As I looked into the water, there were three young dolphins vying for our attention. I did not know them but was learning each of their names when suddenly two larger dolphins swam up from below, displacing the three youngsters. They were Lucky and Hastings! They stared at me, and I stared at them. I wondered if they would remember me after an absence of 31 months. I was so pleased to see them! I looked at my supervisor and asked permission to pet them. He smiled and said, "I think you should do more than that." I glanced back and both Lucky and Hastings had rolled over and were presenting me with their tails.

I joyfully grabbed their tails and played the tail game, exactly as I had played it on my last day with them several years earlier. My supervisor shook his head and said, "We can continue the tour later, you should stay here. I haven't seen them play that game since you left." As he walked away, I welled up with tears. It meant so much to me to be reunited with Lucky and Hastings, my first real teachers. I was happy to be back, and I think Lucky and Hastings felt the same.

I share this story with people whenever they ask me if animals remember their trainers, because there was no question that Lucky and Hastings remembered me. Over the years, I have encountered many examples of the special relationships trainers form with animals, and I have seen it with many different species. Let me share one more dolphin example.

Sortudo, Joaquim, and Carolina

A few years ago, I was attending a training conference in Portugal and a group of us had an opportunity to visit the Lisbon Zoo. The zoo's marine mammal team wanted to demonstrate their latest educational programming and invited us to watch a private session. One of the trainers, Marcia, proudly described the training she had done with three of their dolphins, Sortudo, Joaquim, and Carolina. We gathered around as Marcia blew her whistle and waited for the three dolphins to pop up for the training session.

One of the dolphins, Carolina, poked her head above the water in front of Marcia, ready to go, but the other two dolphins positioned themselves in front of our group and stared at us. Marcia was embarrassed and explained that we must be a distraction. She insisted that she had prepared them for visitors, but she asked us to move to another location where the dolphins are more accustomed to seeing visitors. As we moved, the two uncooperative dolphins watched our group of 12 people and followed us to our new location. Marcia blew her whistle again to start the session. Carolina came right to her, but the other two dolphins seemed fixated on our group. The trainer apologized profusely, but all of us in the group were animal people so we understood and assured her no apology was needed.

We offered to go back to the conference room, and she could tell us more about her project there. But she insisted on trying again. She asked us to back up a bit further so that we weren't as close. As we moved, it was clear that these two dolphins were keenly interested in every move our group made; they had no interest in paying attention to Marcia. We discussed whether one of us was wearing something unusual or if we had any electronics on that were making noises that we just couldn't hear. We tried to help a frustrated Marcia problem-solve. As we changed positions and locations, one of the more observant members of our group commented, "They're looking at Ken!"

I quickly, and somewhat defensively, said, "No, they're looking at the group. Why would they look at me?"

Another member of our group commented, "They *are* looking at Ken!"

Marcia's interest was piqued, and she asked, "Ken, can you move away from the group? Walk around to the other side of the habitat." She pointed to a location far away from her and a good distance from the group.

I immediately started walking away from the group, still skeptical that I was at fault. But to my surprise, the two dolphins followed me and kept staring at me. All I could think to say was, "This is creepy. I am so sorry, Marcia."

"It's like Joaquim and Sortudo know you!" exclaimed Marcia.

I was embarrassed that I had messed up her session but had no explanation about why. "I don't know these dolphins. I've never met them. In fact, this is my first visit to this zoo."

"These two dolphins are here on a breeding loan," explained Marcia. "They are from the United States! We changed their names when they arrived to make it easier for local kids to relate to them."

Suddenly I had dozens of questions, "Where are they from? What are their original names? Can I come closer and look at them?" I came right up to the persistent dolphins and saw a twinkle of recognition in their eyes. There was something familiar, but what was it? I had worked with so many animals in my career. Seeing two dolphins in Lisbon was so completely out of context. I started looking for body marks and other signs that might help me determine if I knew these two dolphins. Then I saw a familiar scar, one that had come from a net entanglement many decades earlier.

Just as I realized exactly who the dolphins were, Marcia said, "Sortudo was called Lucky and Joaquim was called Hastings."

I have no idea what I said at that moment, but I know I must have let out an unbelieving cry! I did not know what to do. I am very respectful of not interacting with someone else's animals without permission, but it took everything in me to keep from jumping into the water with them. Marcia called me away from the water and asked me to come with her. She told everyone else to wait where they were. We went back in the office and Marcia began speaking to her supervisor in Portuguese; it was an animated discussion. Finally, her supervisor took me to the locker room, gave me a wetsuit, and asked if I wanted to do a session with Joaquim and Sortudo (Hastings and Lucky). He had barely gotten the words out of his mouth, before I was half undressed and jumping into that wetsuit.

As I came out to the habitat, Marcia explained to the group that she would work with Carolina and I would work with Sortudo and Joaquim. I was trembling with excitement. I explained to everyone that I had not seen these two dolphins in more than 17 years. I asked Marcia what I should do with them; I did not know any of their current cues. Her supervisor then interjected, "Do whatever you want and let's see what they remember!"

"Let's see what I remember!" I said back to him. "Really, you're okay if I try cues from my time with them?" He nodded yes, and I asked again, "Cues from nearly two decades ago?" He nodded his head vigorously.

I stepped down onto a ledge with water up to my waist. I now could see the familiar shapes of Lucky's body and Hasting's face; the look in their eyes was so obvious to me now. They were older and larger, but then so was I. I tossed them each a fish and presented a simple target cue; both dolphins touched my outstretched palms eagerly. I gave them a pec-slap cue, and they both did that instantly. I asked them to vocalize; they responded immediately. I then got brave and presented an upside-down swim cue. I may have been hesitant and uncertain about the cue, but they were not: they performed the behavior instantly. I cued five or six additional behaviors that I could remember, oblivious to the comments of the group watching or the crowd of trainers from the zoo that had gathered to observe.

Finally, I looked at Marcia and said, "This is incredible. I can't remember any more of their cues!"

"That's OK," she said, "This is amazing."

I had ignored Lucky and Hasting for just a few seconds. I had stopped giving them cues. Suddenly, Lucky swam underwater and lifted his tail, presenting it in front of my face! "The tail game!" I shouted in surprise. I grabbed his tail and started playing the game that I had first taught him more than 25 years earlier. Hastings had a look of recognition on his face and presented his tail, too. The zoo staff let me play with the dolphins for another 30 minutes. As I played the game, I explained the history of the game and my history with both dolphins to everyone watching.

I have experienced many special moments in my career, and it is hard to pick just one that stands out above the others. But this experience was special. It demonstrated for me the power and importance of relationships. But not just for me—the relationship was clearly meaningful to Lucky and Hastings as well. I will never forget my experiences with Lucky and Hastings. I always strive to create the strongest relationship possible with every animal I train.

My Favorite Training and Behavior Books

I love to read. I am old-school and enjoy having a physical library at my fingertips. Often students ask for recommendations about books to add to their libraries or want the best resource to deal with an issue, so I created a list that I hand out to all students who take classes from me. Depending on a student's interest and skill level, I suggest different books. I believe that good recommendations should come with explanations. Trainers don't need every book on my list, so I like to explain why I am making each recommendation to help students, and now readers of this book, choose the right reference for their needs.

This is a list of my favorite training and behavior books; it does not include articles, journals, videos, or websites. Those alternative resources can also provide excellent information, but that will have to be a list for another day (or another book). I've divided this list into the following sections:

- General Behavior Science References
- Focused Behavior Science
- General Positive Reinforcement and Clicker Training
- Puppy Training
- Dealing with Aggression, Fear, and Anxiety
- Training for Sports and Competition
- Husbandry and Medical Training
- Enrichment
- Beyond Dogs
- Training and Teaching People
- Other Valuable Resources

General Behavior Science

There are dozens of excellent resources that you can turn to when it comes to solid science references. It seems that each of us who wants a good reference will pick different go-to resources. Here are my top three.

Chance, P. (2013) *Learning and Behavior,* 7th edition. Cengage Learning.

Chance is my favorite go-to resource when it comes to looking for information about the science. His information is no different than that in any other reference, but he presents it in a more accessible manner. I often suggest this book as the best behavior science reference for the non-scientist.

Kazdin, A. (2012) *Behavior Modification in Applied Settings,* 7th edition. Waveland Press.

This is a standard behavior reference book.

Pierce, W.D. & Cheney, C.D. (2017) *Behavior Analysis and Learning,* 6th edition. Routledge: Taylor and Francis Group.

This is a more recent reference and covers many of the same topics as the others, but it also includes newer information. I always suggest having a reference that is as current as possible, to ensure that you are using the most up-to-date science.

Focused Behavior Science

Miklosi, A. (2007) *Dog Behaviour, Evolution, and Cognition.* Oxford University Press.

This book is unique in that it focuses on dogs and looks at the newer scientific discoveries from the last few decades leading up to its publication.

Schneider, S. (2012) *The Science of Consequences: How They Affect Genes, Change the Brain, and Impact Our World.* Prometheus Books.

This book offers a great review of what is known about consequences, including how and why they work, and recent discoveries about the topic.

Sidman, M. (1989) *Coercion and its Fallout.* Revised edition. Authors Cooperative, Inc., Publishers.

This is one of the only books out there that looks at the challenges of punishment and the impacts that it has on learners.

General Positive Reinforcement and Clicker Training

Alexander, M. (2003). *Click for Joy! Questions and Answers from Clicker Trainers and their Dogs.* Sunshine Books, Inc.

This type of book appeals to me because it takes common questions, concerns, and misconceptions about clicker training and positive reinforcement training and gives clear answers and explanations. There may not be new information here for the experienced trainer, but it is a great resource for new trainers, and I often point clients and students to Melissa's answers.

Laurence, K. (2010). *Clicker Training: The Perfect Foundation.* Sunshine Books, Inc.

Kay is a gifted and innovative trainer. I would probably recommend any book she writes about training. This one offers a great introduction to clicker training from Kay's unique perspective.

Laurence, K. (2009). *Teaching with Reinforcement for Every Day and in Every Way.* Sunshine Books, Inc.

Here Kay looks at reinforcement from new perspectives that will stretch many trainers' understanding of the various types of reinforcement that are available to us.

Pryor, K. (1999). *Don't Shoot the Dog: The New Art of Teaching and Training.* Revised edition. Bantam Books.

Not only was this the first book to expose me to a formal explanation about the value of focusing on positive reinforcement, it is a book that still resonates with me today.

Pryor, K. (2014). *On My Mind: Reflections on Animal Behavior and Learning.* Sunshine Books, Inc.

Karen offers more gems in this great collection of essays that she has written over the years on a wide variety of topics.

Ramirez, K. ed. (2016). *Better Together: The Collected Wisdom of Modern Trainers.* Sunshine Books, Inc.

How could I not recommend this book? I collected 60 articles written by some of the leaders in the positive reinforcement world and put them together because I believe these articles contain useful information for trainers at every level.

Puppy Training

Martin, K. & Martin, D. (2011). *Puppy Start Right: Foundation Training for the Companion Dog.* Sunshine Books, Inc.

This is my favorite book on puppies. It provides clear instructions on raising a puppy with positive reinforcement.

McDevitt, L. (2012). *Control Unleashed: The Puppy Program.* Clean Run Productions, LLC.

I enjoyed Leslie's original *Control Unleashed,* and here she does a great job of taking those lessons and adapting them to work with puppies.

VanArendonk Baugh, L. (2017). *Social, Civil, and Savvy: Training & Socializing Puppies to Become the Best Possible Dogs.* Æclipse Press.

Laura provides another practical guide for puppy owners, written in her unique voice and presented from a positive reinforcement perspective.

Dealing with Aggression, Fear, and Anxiety

Arthur, N. (2009). *Chill Out Fido! How to Calm Your Dog.* Dogwise Publishing.

This is a practical book that is useful for the non-trainer and trainer alike. I particularly like the step-by-step exercises Nan provides to help people work through various common dog problems. This is not a book about aggression, but it focuses on dealing with overly excitable dogs.

DeMartini-Price, M. (2014). *Treating Separation Anxiety in Dogs.* Dogwise Publishing.

Separation anxiety is a common problem for many pet dogs that has stumped the most skilled trainers. Malena's protocol is well-thought-out and practical. Handling these problems usually requires a skilled trainer and behaviorist, and this is a great resource for those professionals.

Donaldson, J. (1996). *The Culture Clash.* James & Kenneth Publishers.

This is one of my go-to references for anyone who wants to understand and deal with aggression. By today's standards, it may be considered an older reference, but the information is not outdated.

Donaldson, J. (2002). *Mine! A Practical Guide to Resource Guarding in Dogs.* Direct Book Service.

The title says it all. This is a short, easy-to-read guide about dealing with resource guarding. I keep buying new copies because I am always giving my copy to friends and clients.

Donaldson, J. (2004). *Fight! A Practical Guide to the Treatment of Dog-Dog Aggression.* Direct Book Service.

For this book, I could repeat what I wrote about Jean's other practical guidebook above.

McDevitt, L. (2007). *Control Unleashed: Creating a Focused and Confident Dog.* Clean Run Productions, LLC.

The opening line on the book's back cover sums it up: "Learn how to turn stress and distraction to focus…" While the book is not about aggression specifically, many of the exercises are good tools for dealing with the issues that cause anxiety, reactivity, and aggression.

McDevitt, L. (2019). *Control Unleashed: Reactive to Relaxed.* First Stone Publishing.

Some might be tempted to suggest that this is just an update of Leslie's original book from 12 years earlier, but it is actually a whole new book presenting new ideas and suggestions for dealing with challenging dogs.

O'Heare, J. (2017). *Aggressive Behavior in Dogs: A Comprehensive Technical Manual for Professionals.* 3rd edition. BehaveTech Publishing.

This is one in a series of books written by Dr. O'Heare that are comprehensive and technically accurate. His books are designed for professionals and serious behaviorists who deal with aggression cases, and not for the casual trainer.

Parsons, E. (2005). *Click to Calm: Healing the Aggressive Dog.* Sunshine Books, Inc.

When I first heard Emma talk about her approach to reinforcing a dog for any reduction in aggressive response and building the desired calm behavior, I was fascinated but skeptical. After watching her work, trying her methods myself, and then reading her book, I found her protocol a truly useful technique for reducing aggression. Although this is not the protocol of choice for every dog or every trainer, there is so much useful information here that anyone who deals with aggression regularly should know this protocol.

Sternberg, S. (2017). *Assessing Aggression Thresholds in Dogs: Using the Assess-A-Pet Protocol to Better Understand Aggression.* Dogwise Publishing.

This is not a book on aggression treatment but a book focused on assessing and understanding aggression. Sue Sternberg is well-known for her assessment protocols, and this book puts her knowledge and protocols together in one useful manual.

Stewart, G. (2016). *Behavior Adjustment Training 2.0: New Practical Techniques for Fear, Frustration, and Aggression in Dogs.* Dogwise Publishing.

Grisha's unique, integrated approach to dealing with reactive dogs takes skill and experience to apply well, but the techniques are worth mastering. Grisha has refined her BAT protocol over the years, and this newest iteration helps trainers give dogs more control over the outcome of their interactions with the world. This is a particularly useful book for people who can work with their own dogs or clients' dogs in big, open spaces such as a park, a field, or a forest.

VanArendonk Baugh, L. (2013). *Fired Up, Frantic, and Freaked Out: Training the Crazy Dogs from Over-the-Top to Under Control.* AEclipse Press.

Like several of the books in this section that I recommend, this is not a book specifically about aggression, but it focuses on many attributes, such as fear, excitement, and nervousness, that can end up in an aggressive behavior. Laura takes a practical, step-by-step approach that clearly comes from many years of working through client challenges.

Training for Sports and Competition

Bertilsson, E. & Johnson Vegh, E. (2010). *Agility Right from the Start: The ultimate training guide to America's fastest-growing dog sport.* Sunshine Books, Inc.

I am not an agility competitor, but I do enjoy watching agility, and I have tried my hand at teaching many of the exercises. As I wrote in the foreword to Eva's and Emelie's book, I love the way they approach the subject with a look at many different exercises. They always ask three questions: "What does the behavior look like?" "How do you train it?" and "What could go wrong?" This is a practical look at using positive reinforcement in the best possible way for agility, and it is useful for many other sports as well.

Branigan, H. (2019). *Awesome Obedience: A Positive Training Plan for Competition Success.* Sunshine Books, Inc.

This is another sport that I know little about, but I do know good training when I see it. I have watched Hannah train and teach for several years now, and she takes a fresh approach to an old sport. Obedience may be the title of the sport because of its roots in traditional training, but the way she trains it is more like awesome fun, awesome cooperation, or awesome game-play. Many of her practical tips are useful in all areas of training.

Fenzi, D, and Jones, D. (2013-2016). *Dog Sports Skills, Books 1-4.* Fenzi Dog Sports Academy Publishing.

The sub-titles of the four books in this series are *1: Developing Engagement & Relationship, 2: Motivation, 3: Play!,* and *4: Focus and Engage!* I might not have read this series had Denise and Deb not asked me to write the foreword to the second book on motivation. After that, I was hooked and I read them all. This series has great training information even for those not involved in competitive dog sports.

Husbandry and Medical Training

This is an important topic for me and one that I get called on to lecture about often in the zoological world. For years, however, I lamented the lack of resources and acceptance of husbandry training with pets. I am glad to see the trend is changing.

Becker, M., Radosta, L, Sung, W., and Becker M. (2018). *From Fearful to Fear Free: A Positive Program to Free Your Dog from Anxiety, Fears, and Phobias.* Health Communications, Inc.

The Fear Free movement is sweeping across the country. It focuses on getting veterinary practices to adopt a kinder, positive reinforcement approach to working with their clients. This is an attractive book with great information about how to recognize fear, the importance of training, and how to be successful at training. It is a great resource for introducing people to the importance and value of husbandry training.

Howell, A. and Feyrecilde, M. (2018). *Cooperative Veterinary Care.* Wiley-Blackwell.

This book is written by two veterinary technicians who specialize in behavior. Who better to describe the challenges of veterinary medical care and propose training solutions for our dogs and cats? An excellent resource for veterinary professionals, it contains great descriptions of how to train some of the most important pet medical behaviors.

Jones, D. (2018). *Cooperative Care: Seven Steps to Stress-Free Husbandry.* K9 in Focus.

This is a straightforward book designed to help dog owners prepare their dogs for less stressful veterinary care. Since most husbandry training books are designed for the animal-care professional, practical tools and good instruction for the non-trainer make this a unique book.

Oblasser-Mirtl, A. and Glatz, B. (2016) *Medical Training for Dogs.* Cadmos Publishing.

This is not an English-language book since it was written by two talented trainers from the Animal Training Center in Austria. But even if you cannot read the book, there are associated videos that are available online and worth checking out.

Overall, K. (2013). *Manual of Clinical Behavioral Medicine for Dogs and Cats.* Elsevier, Inc.

This is a great resource for understanding how veterinary behaviorists deal with pet behavioral problems. This manual is not a substitute for working with veterinary behaviorists, but I like it because it is a good reference about the scope of their work. It can also help trainers recognize when they should reach out to a veterinary behavior specialist.

Ramirez, K. (2013). "Husbandry Training." In *Zookeeping: An Introduction to the Science and Technology,* eds.: Irwin, M.D., Stone, J.B., and Cobaugh, A.M. University of Chicago Press.

This is a large, expensive textbook that not everyone might be able to afford, but it addresses many excellent topics that zoo professionals will find useful. All trainers will find the sections on training, husbandry, and enrichment beneficial.

Shaw, J. and Martin, D. eds. (2015). *Canine and Feline Behavior for Veterinary Technicians and Nurses.* Wiley-Blackwell.

This is another great resource compiled by two veterinary technicians who are also skilled teachers and exceptional trainers. They sought out leading veterinary and behavior experts to write various chapters, providing a rich resource for anyone interested in improved veterinary training.

Yin, S. (2009). *Low Stress Handling, Restraint, and Behavior Modification of Dogs & Cats: Techniques for Developing Patients Who Love Their Visits.* CattleDog Publishing.

The title of the book accurately describes the subject matter of the book and the accompanying DVD. This reference provides good behavioral information, but its biggest value is in demonstrating the best way to manage, handle, and restrain dogs and cats in the veterinary clinic. It is richly illustrated, and techniques are explained in detail. Sophia has left us with an invaluable resource.

Enrichment

One important area of behavior management that has developed in the zoological community is a focus on environmental and behavioral enrichment. Enrichment can make a significant difference in an animal's quality of life and is a topic that is just as important for pets as it is for animals in the zoo. There are only a few excellent resources that focus on this topic; here are the ones I most strongly recommend.

Bender, A. and Strong, E. (2019). *Canine Enrichment for the Real World: Making it a Part of Your Dog's Daily Life.* Dogwise Publishing.

I cannot give this book enough high praise. Not only is it the rare book that focuses on enrichment for dogs, but it does so in a very holistic and practical way. It provides great information about giving animals choice, assessing an animal's needs, and evaluating effectiveness and offers practical tips for implementing enrichment. It combines science and practice beautifully.

Markowitz, H. (1981). *Behavioral Enrichment in the Zoo.* Van Nostrand Reinhold.

Hal Markowitz is considered the father of enrichment. He was one of the first to propose that animals needed to be given the opportunity to exhibit behaviors key to their species, so this is an important historical reference.

Nicassio-Hiskey, N. and Mitchell, C. (2013). *Beyond Squeaky Toys: Innovative ideas for eliminating problem behaviors and enriching the lives of dogs and cats.* Smart Pets Press, LLC.

The zoological world has focused on enrichment for decades, but it has been a more recent development in the pet community. Nicole and Cynthia come from the zoo world and apply their knowledge and understanding of enrichment to creating innovative ideas for dogs and cats.

Shepherdson, D.J., Mellen, J.D., and Hutchins, M. (1998). *Second Nature: Environmental Enrichment for Captive Animals.* Smithsonian Institution Press.

This is a great reference for zoo professionals with contributions from nearly 40 authors.

Young, R.J. (2003). *Environmental Enrichment for Captive Animals.* Wiley-Blackwell.

This is a good resource for zoo professionals new to enrichment. The final chapter titled "Information Sources about Environmental Enrichment" is especially useful.

Beyond Dogs

I have spent a large part of my career working with every species imaginable. We constantly need to remind people that positive training techniques are not just dog-training techniques. They are teaching techniques, behavior-change techniques, and they work with any animal.

Bradshaw, J. and Ellis, S. (2016) *The Trainable Cat: A Practical Guide to Making Life Happier for You and Your Cat.* Basic Books.

This is a well-written book that I enjoyed. It gives those skeptical about cat training clear insights about why training is so beneficial and guides those who want to train a cat toward the best way to get started.

Heidenreich, B. (2004). *Good Bird! A Guide to Solving Behavior Problems in Companion Parrots!* Avian Publications.

Barbara is a skilled and talented trainer whose book helps parrot owners deal with some of the common parrot issues. There are not many bird-training books out there and even fewer written by a positive reinforcement trainer.

Karen Pryor Clicker Training has published a series of books on how to start training a wide variety of common pet species. All of these books give pet owners a great foundation and clear direction about how to start training.

Johnson, M. (2011). *Getting Started: Clicker Training for Birds.* Sunshine Books, Inc.

Kurland, A. (2007). *Clicker Training for Your Horse.* Sunshine Books, Inc.
Alex has led the introduction of clicker training into the horse world. She has several books and many DVDs that are all excellent resources, but I wanted to recommend this great starter book.

Orr, J. and Lewin, T. (2006). *Getting Started: Clicking with Your Rabbit.* Sunshine Books, Inc.

Pryor, K. (2001). *Getting Started: Clicker Training for Cats.* Sunshine Books, Inc.

Ramirez, K. (1999). *Animal Training: Successful Animal Management through Positive Reinforcement.* Sunshine Books, Inc.
I originally designed this book as a comprehensive guide to becoming a professional trainer of any species. Aimed primarily at zoo and aquarium trainers, it became the textbook for a graduate course I taught at Western Illinois University for 20 years, and it is still in use by many trainers. I am hoping to update it and create a new edition, but, until then, it still serves as a useful resource for trainers.

Stafford, G. (2007). *ZOOmility: Keeper Tales of Training with Positive Reinforcement.* iReinforce.com.
Grey is an excellent trainer and teacher who has worked for years in the zoological community. His is a practical guide and an easy read for the new keeper or trainer.

Training and Teaching People

This is an area that animal trainers often overlook. Many of the techniques are the same, but most of us don't know how to translate those skills from animals to our colleagues, clients, and family. Here are the resources that I have found most valuable.

Blanchard, K., Lacinak, T., Tompkins, C., and Ballard, J. (2002). *Whale Done! The Power of Positive Relationships.* The Free Press.

The authors wrote this book for businesses as a lesson in how to improve productivity with positive reinforcement. They use the story of visiting SeaWorld and watching the trainers work with killer whales to explain why these training techniques work with people. Most animal trainers will be able to relate to this story's use of "animal training tools" with people.

Blanchard, K., Lacinak, T., Tompkins, C., and Ballard, J. (2009). *Whale Done Parenting: How to Make Parenting a Positive Experience for You and Your Kids.* Berrett-Koehler Publishers, Inc.

Because of the success of their book *Whale Done!*, the authors followed it up with this excellent look at the use of positive reinforcement tools in raising children.

Covey, S. (2004). *The 7 Habits of Highly Effective People.* Simon & Schuster.

Although this practical and popular bestseller is not a book about positive reinforcement, it uses many aspects of positive reinforcement in the lessons about how to work with people more effectively.

Daniels, A. (2016). *Bringing Out the Best in People: How to Apply the Astonishing Power of Positive Reinforcement.* 3rd edition. McGraw-Hill, Inc.

This book focuses on organizational success through good use of positive reinforcement. The book has remained in print for more than 20 years because of its useful concepts.

Daniels, A. (2009). *Oops! 13 Management Practices that Waste Time and Money (and what to do instead).* Performance Management Publications.

The title says it all. Aubrey Daniels is a skilled behavior analyst with a proven track record of helping businesses improve through better use of behavior analysis principles, especially positive reinforcement.

McKeon, T. (2018). *Don't Nag… TAG! Success the First Time with TAGteach.* TAGteach, LLC.

TAGteach is the remarkable use of a clicker to help shape physical skills with people. I was thrilled when Theresa finally wrote a book about this great concept.

Patterson, K., Grenny, J., McMillan, R., and Switzler, A. (2011). *Crucial Conversations: Tools for Talking When Stakes Are High.* 2nd edition. McGraw-Hill Education.

Probably the hardest time to put training skills to use with people is when you are in a tough conversation. This book focuses on how to have those conversations in the most productive way. It is a must-read for supervisors, coaches, or anyone who must navigate hard conversations.

Ryan, T. (2018). *Coaching People to Train their Dogs*, 2nd edition. Legacy Canine Behavior and Training, Inc.

Terry has great experience as a skilled teacher of trainers. She has translated that knowledge into this excellent book, a valuable resource for anyone who is teaching classes or coaching clients.

Ryan, T. (2017). *Gamify Your Dog Training: Training Games for Group Instruction.* Dogwise Publishing.

Here Terry has collected creative games for use in training classes.

Vargas, J. (2013). *Behavior Analysis for Effective Teaching.* 2nd edition. Routledge.

Julie, B.F. Skinner's daughter, is a behavior analyst who uses the science of behavior to help the reader become a better teacher.

Other Valuable Resources

Here are some books that I like that don't necessarily fit into the categories above, yet I recommend these titles frequently.

Burch, M. and Bailey, J. (1999). *How Dogs Learn.* Howell Book House.

This is a book with great scientific information focused specifically on its application to dog training. I like that it makes the science more accessible to the average dog trainer.

Case, L. (2014). *Beware the Straw Man: The Science Dog Explores Dog Training Fact & Fiction.* AutumnGold Publishing.

I am a fan of Linda's writing. She does not take anything at face value, she investigates common beliefs or statements about training, and she looks at the facts so that she can either support or contradict these popular ideas. This is a great resource and a great read.

Case, L. (2018). *Dog Smart: Evidence-based Training with The Science Dog.* AutumnGold Publishing.

A follow-up to Linda's previous book, this one focuses on new beliefs and new information, all supported with scientific evidence.

Horowitz, A. (2009). *Inside of a Dog: What Dogs See, Smell, and Know.* Scribner.

Dr. Horowitz is a cognitive scientist who does a great job looking at the world from a dog's point of view. Here she provides a good read with great information.

Laurence, K. (2008). *Learning Games.* Sunshine Books, Inc.

Kay focuses on creative games that you can play with your dog to expand his skills and learning. I highly recommend this book for people interested in doing cognitive training with their dogs.

Lindsay, S. (2000, 2001, 2005). *Handbook of Applied Dog Behavior and Training, Volumes 1-3.* Blackwell Publishing and Iowa State University Press.

This well-researched series provides useful information for any dog-behavior professional in every volume. Volume 1: *Etiology and Assessment of Behavior Problems*, Volume 2: *Adaptation and Learning*, and Volume 3: *Procedures and Protocols.*

McConnell, P. (2007). *For the Love of a Dog: Understanding Emotion in You and Your Best Friend.* Ballantine Books.

I love Patricia McConnell's writing and her thoughtful approach to dog behavior. I recommend reading everything she has written. This is one of my favorites.

Pryor, K. (1995). *On Behavior: Essays and Research.* Sunshine Books, Inc.

In this collection of Karen's writings, you can open to any article and find an enjoyable essay with good information.

Pryor, K. (2004). *Lads Before the Wind: Diary of a Dolphin Trainer.* Expanded edition. Sunshine Books, Inc.

This book was my first introduction to Karen. I was a young dolphin trainer, and here was someone who had entered the field with little experience working with marine mammals, a background I could relate to. The book is funny, informative, inspirational—and holds a sentimental place in my heart.

Pryor, K. (2009). *Reaching the Animal Mind: Clicker Training and What it Teaches Us about All Animals.* Scribner.

This is one of Karen's most recent books, and, like all of her volumes, it is a fascinating read.

Sdao, K. (2012). *Plenty in Life Is Free: Reflections on Dogs, Training and Finding Grace.* Dogwise Publishing.

Kathy is a great trainer and speaker whose perspective I appreciate. Her first book really speaks to the ethics of training in a logical and non-preachy way.

Acknowledgements

Producing a collection of essays and stories like the ones in this book would not be possible without the help and encouragement of many people. I am indebted to my colleagues, clients, family, and friends who have always inspired me to do what I love—helping people train better. But I am also eternally grateful to the animals I have had the good fortune of meeting, training, and helping throughout my career. My work has been for them and my learning is because of them.

I would like to start by thanking Karen Pryor, whom I first met in 1990, but who had inspired me many years earlier when I read her book *Lads Before the Wind*. Her invitation to participate in ClickerExpo in 2002 started me on a journey of incredible growth. After Karen's 80th birthday, she decided it was time to slow down and possibly retire. She invited me to step into her role at Karen Pryor Clicker Training, a humbling offer. It is a role that I have taken very seriously since 2014. I owe so much of the growth represented in the stories in this book to what I have learned from Karen and to the opportunities she has provided me.

During the five years when many of these essays were written, there were key people in my life who were instrumental in giving me guidance, assistance, and inspiration. I am indebted to Lisa Takaki for her help as I made the transition from the Shedd Aquarium in Chicago to The Ranch in Washington; she partnered with me to create the Karen Pryor National Training Center. Equally helpful to me during this period were Julie Ramirez, Aaron Clayton, Lori Chamberland, Lilly Strassberg, Gretchen Carey, Lindsay Wood Brown, Shelly Brouwer, Susan Friedman, Jesse and Lili Chavez, Bruce Jorgansun, Jerry Mitchell, and Ilana Alderman. I must single out Ilana (and, by extension, Rob and Ethan for being patient and supportive) for her invaluable contributions to the essays in this book and to my growth as a teacher. She is a wonderful thought partner who challenges my thinking, discusses and debates concepts, and polishes and improves my essays regularly.

It is hard to single out the many talented trainers I have met and worked with over the years, people who have inspired and taught me along the way. They include the faculty of Karen Pryor Academy, the faculty and speakers at ClickerExpo, the members of IMATA (International Marine Animal Trainers Association), members of ABMA (Animal Behavior Managers Alliance), and the staff of the Shedd Aquarium in Chicago.

Finally, I want to thank Julie Gordon for her leadership in bringing this book to fruition and Nini Bloch and Marie Clougher for their thoughtful editing, ensuring that the content of *The Eye of the Trainer* will be understandable to future readers.

About the Author

As the Executive Vice-President (EVP) and Chief Training Officer of Karen Pryor Clicker Training (KPCT), Ken Ramirez develops courses and programming for the Karen Pryor Academy and The Ranch (the Karen Pryor National Training Center) in the state of Washington.

A 40+-year veteran of animal care and training, Ken is a biologist and animal behavior specialist who has overseen or consulted on zoo training projects globally, including 25+ years as EVP of Animal Care and Animal Training at Chicago's Shedd Aquarium. There he developed and supervised animal care, staff training, and public presentation programs for more than 32,000 animals. A prolific and popular author, Ken wrote *Animal Training: Successful Animal Management through Positive Reinforcement*, and taught a graduate course on animal training at Western Illinois University for 20 years.

Ken began his training career working with guide dogs for the visually impaired. He continues to work with organizations training dogs for service work, search-and-rescue, bomb detection, and narcotic detection, consults on zoological projects, and pursues innovations in the fields of pet training and wildlife behavior management.